# MY PETITE KITCHEN
# COOKBOOK

# MY PETITE KITCHEN COOKBOOK

## SIMPLE WHOLEFOOD RECIPES

### ELEANOR OZICH

MURDOCH BOOKS

# CONTENTS

# INTRODUCTION

'Simple' is a word not often honoured in today's busy lives. However, it was this very word that inspired me to start writing a daily recipe blog. Petite Kitchen was created purely to share my passion and vision for wholesome, nourishing food. Every recipe in this book encapsulates my experiences of personal research, trial and testing, resulting in each recipe being created as nature intended it to be — simple!

The road to simple eating began when our daughter, Izabella, developed a severe skin condition. Despite countless visits to doctors and specialists, nobody could shine light on her condition, or explain the impact it had on her behaviour. In despair, we visited a naturopath, who explained Izabella was suffering from an imbalance of bad gut bacteria, causing toxins that were resulting in her skin condition, among other issues. This revelation made complete sense to me.

We decided to embark on an exciting new journey, to heal and nourish our bodies, not only for our daughter, but also for ourselves. We removed gluten and almost all grains, all refined sugar, additives and preservatives from our diets, and adopted a simple and clean way of eating that our generation seems to have lost sight of.

This beautiful, natural diet has helped our little girl in ways I can't even explain. The impact it has had on my husband, my one-year-old son and of course myself has been almost unbelievable. Energy, positivity and a new lease of life now grace our home.

*My Petite Kitchen Cookbook* is the lovingly nurtured result of this transformation. It is inspiring that food — the very item that is causing obesity, depression and health epidemics of unfathomable proportions — is also the very thing that can be used to cure, cleanse and help our bodies and minds.

The recipes in this book work wonderfully in all seasons and for all occasions, and can be enjoyed by the whole family. Each and every recipe is lovingly selected, and contains whole, natural and unprocessed ingredients, so that you can enjoy life's delicious pleasures, while also nourishing your body.

I believe food truly brings people together. It is something so special and beautiful to be shared with others, and should be made with plenty of love and care.

Enjoy, look and ask, but most of all, I invite you to taste. Get lost for an afternoon in your kitchen. This is the essence of my mission — to provide others with the joy and happiness that has graced our little family.

Eleanor Ozich

# A NOTE FROM THE AUTHOR

I have annotated each recipe, indicating whether it is gluten-free, dairy-free, suitable for vegetarians, or for vegans, or a combination of these. When a recipe is not gluten-free, I have suggested an alternative ingredient to make it so.

The recipes are coded as follows:

GF: Gluten-free
DF: Dairy-free
VEG: Suitable for vegetarians
V: Suitable for vegans

# BREAKFAST

Breakfast is a cherished time in our family. Sitting around the breakfast bar and enjoying a meal together is the perfect way to prepare for the day ahead.

The recipes gathered here vary from those that can be prepared the night before, such as Coconut bircher muesli and Chia seed breakfast pudding, to comforting staples such as Apple, nutmeg and buckwheat porridge, and my personal favourites, Shallot and thyme frittata and a wonderful Mushroom soufflé omelette – perfect for enjoying on a lazy weekend morning.

I love adding new textures and flavours to classic breakfast recipes, so feel free to add a scattering of your own favourite dried fruits, shredded coconut, crushed nuts or seeds to your creations. Whatever your morning breakfast style, I'm sure you'll find a wholesome recipe or two here to tickle your fancy.

# EGG POTS WITH NUTMEG CRÈME FRAÎCHE

*These insanely delicious egg pots are super simple to make. They're almost like a toasted sandwich, but in muffin form, with a delicious runny poached egg inside. Our kids absolutely love them.*

*This version is vegetarian, but it is also divine with some prosciutto or cooked bacon added.*

**SERVES 6** ❖ GF, VEG

125 g (4½ oz/½ cup) crème fraîche, or 125 ml (4 fl oz/ ½ cup) thin (pouring) cream
2 tablespoons dijon mustard
½ teaspoon freshly grated nutmeg
6 slices of gluten-free bread
3 tablespoons melted ghee, butter or olive oil
6 free-range eggs
1 small handful of thyme leaves or chopped flat-leaf (Italian) parsley

Preheat the oven to 180°C (350°F/Gas 4).

Put the crème fraîche, mustard and nutmeg in a small bowl with a pinch of sea salt and freshly ground black pepper. Beat well with a whisk, then set aside.

Flatten each slice of bread with a rolling pin, then brush each side with the melted ghee. Line six standard muffin holes with the bread, pressing them in carefully with your hands so they don't tear.

Carefully crack an egg into each bread case, then spoon about 2 tablespoons of the crème fraîche mixture over each. Sprinkle with the herbs.

Bake for 15–20 minutes, depending on how you like your eggs cooked. Serve immediately.

# CHEDDAR AND QUINOA MUFFINS WITH SUN-DRIED TOMATOES AND BASIL

*Full of wholesome goodness, these warm, savoury quinoa muffins are deliciously cheesy, enriched with the sweetness of sun-dried tomatoes. I like to make a large batch for breakfast, saving some for an afternoon snack. The muffins are also a brilliant addition to a summer picnic.*

**MAKES 6 MEDIUM OR 12 MINI MUFFINS** ❖ GF, VEG

Preheat the oven to 180°C (350°F/Gas 4).

Line the holes of a muffin tin with baking paper. If making six medium muffins, line six holes of a standard 12-hole muffin tin. Alternatively, line 12 holes of a mini muffin tin.

Put all the ingredients in a large mixing bowl and add a large pinch of sea salt and freshly ground black pepper. Using your hands or a wooden spoon, mix well until combined.

Divide the mixture among the muffin holes and bake for 25 minutes, or until a skewer inserted in the middle of a muffin comes out clean.

## NOTE ▰▰▰

If you don't have any left-over cooked quinoa, place 150 g (5½ oz/ ¾ cup) rinsed quinoa in a saucepan with 375 ml (13 fl oz/1½ cups) vegetable stock. Bring to a gentle boil over medium heat, then reduce the heat to low. Cover and simmer for 12–15 minutes, or until almost all the liquid has been absorbed. Stir the grains using a fork or spoon, then cover and leave to sit for 10 minutes. You should now have the right amount of cooked quinoa for these muffins.

540 g (1 lb 3 oz/2 cups) cooked quinoa (see Note)

4 free-range eggs, lightly beaten

100 g (3½ oz/1 cup) grated cheddar cheese

2 large handfuls of basil leaves, roughly chopped

40 g (1½ oz/¼ cup) sun-dried tomatoes, finely chopped

# PARMESAN-TOPPED MUSHROOM SOUFFLÉ OMELETTE

*This light, fluffy omelette puffs up to twice its size while baking in the oven, giving off the most delicious smell.*

*I like to serve it with crispy bacon and a lovely green salad for weekend brunch.*

**SERVES 3–4** ❖ GF, VEG

Preheat the oven to 180°C (350°F/Gas 4).

Place the egg whites in a clean bowl with a pinch of salt. Using an electric mixer, beat until stiff peaks form.

In a separate bowl, beat the egg yolks with a whisk for a minute or so, until lighter in colour.

Fold half the beaten egg white into the egg yolk until evenly incorporated. Now fold the remaining egg white through, being careful not to overmix.

Melt the ghee in a large ovenproof frying pan over medium heat. Add the mushrooms, along with a pinch of sea salt and freshly ground black pepper. Sauté for 10 minutes, or until the mushrooms are nicely browned and softened.

Pour in the egg mixture, then scatter the parsley and half the parmesan on top. Place the frying pan in the oven and bake for 5 minutes, or until the omelette has doubled in height.

Sprinkle with the remaining parmesan and the lemon juice, drizzle with olive oil and serve immediately.

6 free-range eggs, separated
2 tablespoons ghee, butter
　　or olive oil
180 g (6 oz/2 cups) thinly
　　sliced portobello
　　mushrooms
1 large handful of flat-leaf
　　(Italian) parsley, roughly
　　chopped
1 large handful of grated
　　parmesan cheese
1 tablespoon lemon juice
extra virgin olive oil, to serve

# HERBED BREAKFAST HASH WITH SWEDE, PANCETTA AND PARMESAN

*This is one of my favourite brunch recipes, and is an excellent way to use up left-over vegetables. I've used roast swede in this recipe, but any left-over roasted root vegetable would work well. You can use other dark leafy greens instead of spinach, and omit the parmesan for a dairy-free version.*

SERVES 2–4 ❖ GF

420 g (15 oz/2 cups) finely chopped left-over roast swede (rutabaga)
6–8 strips of pancetta or prosciutto
2 large handfuls of chopped English spinach leaves
4 free-range eggs
1 handful of fresh herbs, such as basil, flat-leaf (Italian) parsley and chives
50 g (1¾ oz/½ cup) finely grated parmesan cheese
extra virgin olive oil, for drizzling

Preheat the oven to 180°C (350°F/Gas 4).

Heat a large ovenproof frying pan until warmed through. Evenly assemble the swede, pancetta and spinach in the warm pan.

Make four small wells in the mixture, then carefully crack an egg into each hole. Sprinkle the herbs and parmesan on top, then season with sea salt and freshly ground black pepper. Drizzle with a little olive oil.

Bake for 15–20 minutes, depending on how you like your eggs cooked. Serve hot.

# THE BEST BAKED BEANS

*What I love about these deliciously tasty baked beans is that they can be eaten for breakfast, lunch or dinner, and are a total winner with the kids. I swear, once you try these, you'll never buy the tinned version again. Feel free to add your favourite herbs and spices for an extra flavour kick.*

*I like to make a double batch of these baked beans, and reserve some for when I don't feel like cooking.*

SERVES 4 ❖ GF, DF (if no ghee or butter used), VEG (if using vegetable stock), V (if no ghee, butter or chicken stock used)

2 tablespoons ghee, butter or olive oil

1 leek, white part only, cut in half lengthways, then finely chopped

6 garlic cloves, roughly chopped

1 handful of thyme leaves, roughly chopped

1 litre (35 fl oz/4 cups) organic chicken or vegetable stock

125 g (4½ oz/½ cup) tomato paste (concentrated purée)

400 g (14 oz) tin white beans, such as haricot (navy) beans, butterbeans or cannellini beans

Melt the ghee in a large saucepan over medium heat. Add the leek and garlic and sauté for 10 minutes, until soft and slightly browned.

Add the thyme, stock, tomato paste and beans and bring to a gentle boil. Reduce the heat to low and simmer, uncovered, for 35–45 minutes, until the liquid has reduced by half — the sauce should be thick and pulpy.

Season with sea salt and freshly ground black pepper.

The beans will keep for 1 week in an airtight container in the fridge.

# CARAMELISED SHALLOT AND THYME FRITTATA WITH BUFFALO MOZZARELLA

*Honeyed thyme shallots add a subtle sweet and aromatic depth to this tasty frittata. Topped with creamy buffalo mozzarella, it is an absolute pleasure to eat. It is lovely on its own, or add a green salad and call it brunch. It is equally good cold, as a picnic dish.*

**SERVES 2** ❖ GF, VEG

4 tablespoons ghee, butter or olive oil

10 French shallots, roughly chopped

2 handfuls of thyme leaves, roughly chopped, plus extra sprigs to garnish

2 tablespoons honey, or maple or agave syrup

4 free-range eggs, lightly beaten

150 g (5½ oz) fresh buffalo mozzarella, roughly torn

Preheat the oven to 200°C (400°F/Gas 6).

Melt the ghee in a frying pan over medium heat, until sizzling. Add the shallot, thyme and a pinch of sea salt and freshly ground black pepper. Sauté for 10–12 minutes, until the shallot is soft and slightly browned.

Turn the heat to low and drizzle the honey on top. Continue to cook for 8–10 minutes, stirring every minute or so, until the shallot is lovely and caramelised. You can add a little water if the mixture starts to stick to the bottom of the pan.

Transfer the mixture to a small pie dish, about 375 ml (13 fl oz/1½ cups) in capacity, and spread it out evenly. Pour the beaten eggs over, then top with the mozzarella and extra thyme sprigs.

Bake for 10 minutes, or until the egg is cooked through and slightly golden on top. Serve hot or cold.

- 65 g (2¼ oz/1 cup) shredded coconut
- 75 g (2½ oz/½ cup) dried cranberries (or other dried fruit of your choice)
- 40 g (1½ oz/¼ cup) pepitas (pumpkin seeds)
- 2 tablespoons chia seeds (poppy seeds also work well)
- 65 g (2¼ oz/½ cup) sliced almonds
- 70 g (2½ oz/½ cup) ground seeds or nuts of your choice
- 40 g (1½ oz/¼ cup) sunflower seeds

# RAW SHREDDED COCONUT, CHIA AND ALMOND CEREAL

*This is a lovely coconutty, crunchy, sweet and chewy breakfast cereal. Serve it with milk of your choice, and if you're feeling fancy, an extra dollop of yoghurt, a drizzle of honey and some fresh fruit. You can easily double or triple the quantities if you wish to make more.*

**SERVES 6-8** ❖ GF, DF, VEG, V

Mix all the ingredients together in a large bowl, then transfer to an airtight glass jar.

The cereal will keep in a cool dark place for up to 6 months.

# THE BEST BAKED BANANAS

*The perfect guilt-free breakfast, dessert or even midday treat, these sticky baked bananas are drizzled with honey and lemon juice and spiced with cinnamon. These simple flavours work beautifully together; every mouthful gives an incredible burst of sweet, spicy, syrupy goodness.*

*Serve the bananas topped with a sprinkling of mixed seeds, chopped dried fruit and a dollop of plain yoghurt if desired.*

**SERVES 3–4** ❖ GF, DF, VEG, V (if no honey used)

4 unpeeled bananas, sliced
   in half lengthways
115 g (4 oz/⅓ cup) honey,
   or 80 ml (2½ oz/⅓ cup)
   maple or agave syrup
juice of 1 lemon
2 teaspoons ground
   cinnamon

Preheat the oven to 180°C (350°F/Gas 4).

Lay the bananas, skin side down, on a large baking tray. Drizzle with the honey and lemon juice, then sprinkle with the cinnamon.

Bake for 30–35 minutes, or until nicely golden and caramelised. Serve warm.

# NUT BUTTER DATE BREAD

*This deliciously moist, light and fluffy date bread is made entirely from nutrient-rich, wholesome ingredients, with the nut butter giving it an incredible texture.*

*The bread slices excellently and is wonderful with a large smear of butter and jam.*

**MAKES 10–12 SLICES** ❖ GF, DF, VEG

160 g (5½ oz/1 cup) pitted medjool dates, soaked in water overnight, then drained well

375 g (13 oz/1½ cups) nut butter

4 free-range eggs

1 teaspoon bicarbonate of soda (baking soda)

1 tablespoon apple cider vinegar

1 handful of slivered almonds, for decorating (optional)

Preheat the oven to 150°C (300°F/Gas 2). Line a 22 x 12 cm (8½ x 4½ inch) loaf (bar) tin with baking paper.

Put the dates, nut butter, eggs, bicarbonate of soda and vinegar in a large bowl. Using a potato masher, mash all the ingredients well and mix together until the mixture resembles a smooth paste. (You can also use a food processor to do this, if you prefer.)

Spoon the batter into the tin. If decorating with the almonds, scatter them evenly on top.

Pop into the oven and bake for 40–50 minutes, or until a skewer inserted in the middle of the loaf comes out clean.

Remove from the oven and leave to cool in the tin before inverting onto a wire rack.

The loaf will keep for 3–4 days in an airtight container, and can be frozen for up to 2 months wrapped in foil or plastic wrap.

# COCONUT CREPES WITH BANANA AND MAPLE SYRUP

*Coconut flour gives these sweet, delicious crepes a subtle nutty flavour, and a light texture. Naturally loaded with protein and fibre, this delicious breakfast or brunch will keep you feeling completely satisfied, and may even become your new favourite go-to recipe.*

**SERVES 2** ❖ GF, DF (if no dairy milk or butter used), VEG

45 g (1½ oz/¼ cup) coconut flour
4 free-range eggs
160 ml (5¼ fl oz) Nut milk (page 225), or other milk of your choice
60 ml (2 fl oz/¼ cup) melted extra virgin coconut oil or unsalted butter, plus extra for greasing
2 bananas, sliced into rounds
maple syrup, to serve
shredded coconut, for sprinkling

Put the coconut flour, eggs, milk and coconut oil in a blender with a pinch of sea salt. Process until smooth.

Grease a large frying pan with some extra coconut oil and place over low heat. Carefully pour about 60 ml (2 fl oz/¼ cup) of the batter into the middle of the pan. Cook for 1–2 minutes on each side, until golden brown and slightly fluffy.

Repeat with the remaining batter, keeping the cooked crepes warm. You should end up with four or five crepes.

Fill the crepes with the banana slices. Drizzle with maple syrup, sprinkle with coconut and serve.

# RAW BERRY
# BREAKFAST BOWL

*This raw berry breakfast is beautifully thick, silky and creamy, and contains a secret ingredient — avocado, for a good dose of natural plant fat. I particularly enjoy this breakfast in summer, and love how it makes me feel light and satisfied, yet full of energy to go. The perfect way to start the day.*

**SERVES 2** ❖ GF, DF (if no dairy milk, cream or yoghurt used), VEG,
V (if no dairy or honey used)

250 g (9 oz/2 cups) frozen
  berries
flesh of 1 avocado, roughly
  chopped
juice of 1 lemon
2 tablespoons honey, or
  maple, agave or date syrup
250 ml (9 fl oz/1 cup)
  Nut milk (page 225), or
  other milk of your choice
coconut cream, cream or
  plain yoghurt, to serve

Put the berries, avocado, lemon juice, honey and nut milk in a blender. Process until smooth and creamy, then adjust the sweetness as desired.

Serve in bowls with a swirl of coconut cream, cream or yoghurt.

# CREAMY COCONUT AND CHIA SEED BREAKFAST PUDDING

*Creamy and sweet, this pudding is so full of goodness it can be eaten for breakfast, as a light snack, or even as a silky-sweet dessert. As it has a base of coconut milk, and is sweetened with a touch of honey, it is free from refined sugar, dairy and gluten.*

*What I love most about this pudding is that it does not need to be cooked — simply place all the ingredients in a jar, leave to soak, then enjoy.*

**SERVES 3–4** ❖ GF, DF, VEG, V (if no honey used)

400 ml (14 fl oz) tin coconut milk or coconut cream
35 g (1¼ oz/½ cup) shredded or desiccated coconut
40 g (1½ oz/⅓ cup) chia seeds
2 tablespoons honey, or maple, agave or date syrup
1 teaspoon ground cinnamon, plus extra to serve
1 teaspoon vanilla extract
fresh fruit, to serve

Put the coconut milk, coconut, chia seeds, honey, cinnamon and vanilla in a glass bowl or jar.

Mix well, then place in the fridge and leave to soak overnight, or for at least 2 hours.

Serve topped with fresh fruit and an extra sprinkling of cinnamon.

# BUCKWHEAT PORRIDGE WITH NUTMEG, APPLE AND CRUSHED HAZELNUTS

*This deliciously comforting buckwheat porridge has a surprising yet beautiful texture, with apple and cinnamon enhancing the nutty flavour of the buckwheat. Serve with your favourite berries, and plain yoghurt or milk if desired.*

**SERVES 4** ❖ GF, DF, VEG, V

295 g (10¼ oz/1½ cups) buckwheat
750 ml (26 fl oz/3 cups) water, coconut water, Nut milk (page 225) or Creamy oat milk (page 224)
2 apples, grated
1 teaspoon freshly grated nutmeg
2–3 tablespoons honey, or maple or date syrup
2 tablespoons crushed hazelnuts
fresh or thawed frozen berries, to serve

Rinse the buckwheat in water, then place in a medium saucepan with the water, apple, nutmeg, honey and a pinch of sea salt. Bring to a gentle boil, then reduce the heat to a simmer.

Cook, uncovered, for 20–25 minutes, stirring every so often, until the water is completely absorbed.

Serve warm, sprinkled with the hazelnuts and berries.

# BUCKWHEAT PANCAKES TOPPED WITH ORANGE AND HONEY

*Despite its name, buckwheat is not a variety of wheat, but a type of fruit seed, making it gluten-free, nutritious and energising. These pancakes have a light, airy texture and delicate nutty flavour. They are delicious paired with citrus fruit, and are made for mopping up honey, maple syrup or date syrup.*

**SERVES 2-3** ❖ GF, DF (if no dairy alternatives used), VEG

130 g (4½ oz/1 cup) buckwheat flour (or use half buckwheat flour, and half other gluten-free flour of your choice)

310 ml (10¾ fl oz/1¼ cups) Nut milk (page 225), or other milk of your choice

2 free-range eggs

1 tablespoon honey, or maple or agave syrup, plus extra to serve

1 teaspoon bicarbonate of soda (baking soda)

extra virgin coconut oil, ghee or butter, for greasing

2-3 oranges, peeled, white pith removed, flesh cut into wedges

whipped cream, mascarpone cheese, plain yoghurt or coconut whipped cream, to serve

Put the flour in a large bowl with the nut milk, eggs, honey, bicarbonate of soda and a pinch of sea salt. Beat using an electric mixer until a smooth batter is obtained. (You could also use a blender for this.)

Melt the coconut oil or ghee in a large frying pan over medium heat. Using one large spoonful of batter for each pancake, ladle the batter into the pan — you should have room to cook three pancakes at a time. Cook the pancakes for 1-2 minutes on each side, until lovely and golden.

Repeat with the remaining batter, keeping the cooked pancakes warm. Serve with the orange wedges, whipped cream and some extra honey.

# COCONUT BIRCHER MUESLI

*This muesli is ridiculously easy to make — just place the ingredients in a jar the night before, then wake up to enjoy a deliciously creamy, nourishing breakfast.*

*I've kept this recipe relatively simple, as I feel it doesn't need any fancy ingredients, but feel free to serve it with your favourite dried fruit and a sprinkling of nuts.*

SERVES 2 ❖ GF, DF (if no dairy milk used), VEG, V (if no dairy milk or honey used)

100 g (3½ oz/1 cup) rolled (porridge) oats
375 ml (13 fl oz/1½ cups) coconut cream or milk
35 g (1¼ oz/½ cup) shredded coconut
a drizzle of honey, or maple or date syrup, to serve

Place the oats, coconut cream and coconut in a large jar with a pinch of sea salt. Mix well, then cover and leave in the fridge overnight.

Serve with your favourite fruit, nuts and a drizzle of honey.

# LIGHT MEALS & SIDES

Here's a fabulous assortment of easy dishes, starring simple ingredients to ensure the flavours shine. Each recipe has been created with health in mind, and is designed to tickle the tastebuds.

You'll find plenty of vibrant salads, some tempting soups and delicious vegetable side dishes that can be enjoyed on their own as a light lunch, or as an excellent accompaniment to a main meal.

# SWEET POTATO, CARROT AND CASHEW SOUP

*Golden and slightly sweet, this richly textured soup is very simple to prepare. The cashews lend creaminess, and the garlic adds a lovely kick.*

**SERVES 4** ❖ GF, DF (if served without dairy), VEG (if made using vegetable stock), V (if made using vegetable stock and served without dairy)

3 large orange sweet potatoes, peeled and roughly chopped
3 large carrots, roughly chopped
1.5–2 litres (52–70 fl oz/ 6–8 cups) Home-made vegetable stock (page 207) or chicken stock (page 206)
2 garlic cloves, peeled
2 handfuls of toasted cashew nuts
sour cream, crème fraîche or plain yoghurt, to serve
extra virgin olive oil, for drizzling (optional)

Put the sweet potato and carrot in a stockpot or large saucepan and cover with the stock. Bring to a gentle boil, then reduce the heat and simmer for 30 minutes, or until the vegetables are tender and the liquid has reduced slightly.

Leave to cool for 5 minutes, then transfer to a blender, one ladleful at a time. Add the garlic and most of the cashews, reserving some nuts to garnish the soup. Blend until smooth, then season to taste with sea salt and freshly ground black pepper.

Gently reheat the soup and ladle into bowls. Top with a dollop of sour cream, crème fraîche or yoghurt and the reserved cashews. Serve with an extra sprinkling of black pepper, and a drizzle of olive oil if desired.

# COLD CUCUMBER, MINT AND YOGHURT SOUP

*This cool, minty soup is refreshing on a hot summer's day, and is fabulous as a starter. Light, nourishing and beautiful, it has a subtle tang from the yoghurt and a silky texture from the avocado.*

*To make the soup dairy-free or vegan, use coconut cream instead of yoghurt.*

**SERVES 4** ❖ GF, VEG

2 telegraph (long) cucumbers, peeled, seeds removed, flesh roughly chopped
260 g (9¼ oz/1 cup) plain yoghurt, plus extra to serve
flesh of 2 avocados, roughly chopped
1 large handful of mint leaves, plus extra to garnish

Put the cucumber, yoghurt, avocado and mint in a food processor or blender. Add a pinch of sea salt and freshly ground black pepper and blend until smooth. If the soup is too thick, you can add a little water to adjust the consistency.

Serve chilled, with a swirl of extra yoghurt, a garnish of extra mint leaves and an extra sprinkling of black pepper.

# ROASTED GARLIC AND PARSNIP SOUP

*This fragrant, velvety soup is very nourishing and good for the soul. Roasting the garlic and parsnips beforehand gives a rich, earthy flavour; the parsnips truly shine with the addition of a little lemon and honey.*

*For a vegetarian version, use vegetable stock instead of chicken stock.*

**SERVES 4** ❖ GF, DF

6 parsnips, peeled and
  sliced lengthways
1 garlic bulb, each clove
  peeled and lightly
  smashed
2 tablespoons honey, or
  maple or agave syrup
2 tablespoons extra virgin
  olive oil, plus extra
  for drizzling
750 ml–1 litre (26–35 fl oz/
  3–4 cups) Home-made
  chicken stock (page 206)
juice of ½ lemon
thyme sprigs, to garnish

Preheat the oven to 180°C (350°F/Gas 4).

Arrange the parsnip and garlic cloves on a large baking tray. Drizzle with the honey and olive oil, then season with sea salt and freshly ground black pepper.

Roast for 30–40 minutes, until the vegetables are golden and slightly caramelised.

Transfer the parsnip and garlic cloves to a blender or food processor.

Heat the stock until hot, but not quite simmering. Add half the stock to the roasted vegetables, along with all the lemon juice. Blend until smooth.

Add the remaining stock and blend until the preferred consistency is achieved.

Gently reheat the soup, then ladle into bowls. Drizzle with a little extra olive oil, sprinkle with black pepper, garnish with thyme and serve.

# ARTICHOKE AND GREEN BEAN SALAD WITH TOASTED PINE NUTS

*This salad is best enjoyed warm. It pairs the delicately lovely earthiness of the artichokes with blanched green beans and parsley — a perfect match. The dressing lends a slight tartness, and the toasted pine nuts add a nutty fragrance. Beautiful.*

**SERVES 2** as a light meal, or **4** as a side ❖ GF, VEG

250 g (9 oz) green beans, ends trimmed

340 g (11¾ oz) jar marinated artichokes, drained and roughly chopped

1 large handful of flat-leaf (Italian) parsley, roughly chopped

80 g (2¾ oz/½ cup) toasted pine nuts

### LEMON AND YOGHURT DRESSING

60 ml (2 fl oz/¼ cup) extra virgin olive oil

70 g (2½ oz/¼ cup) plain or Greek-style yoghurt

juice of ½ lemon

To make the dressing, put the olive oil, yoghurt and lemon juice in a small bowl. Add a pinch of sea salt and freshly ground black pepper, mix well and set aside.

Put the beans in a saucepan, cover with water and bring to a gentle boil. Reduce the heat and simmer for 2–3 minutes, or until just cooked. Drain, then allow to cool slightly.

Put the beans, artichokes and parsley in a large salad bowl. Add the dressing and toss until well coated. Scatter the pine nuts on top and serve immediately.

# SMOKED SALMON SALAD WITH HORSERADISH CREAM AND DILL

*This salad is definitely one of my favourites, especially when having guests over for a meal. The smoked salmon pairs fantastically with the peppery rocket and dill. With each mouthful, you get a lovely zing from the lemon and a good strong bite from the creamy horseradish sauce. A perfectly glorious salad.*

3 large handfuls of rocket
  (arugula)
200 g (7 oz) smoked salmon
3 tablespoons thick (double)
  cream or plain yoghurt
3 tablespoons bottled or
  fresh grated horseradish
juice of 1 lemon
a good drizzle of extra virgin
  olive oil
1 small handful of dill

**SERVES 2** as a light meal, or **4** as a side ❖ GF

Arrange the rocket and salmon on a large salad platter — I like to roll the salmon into little rolls before placing them on the leaves.

In a small bowl, mix together the cream and horseradish. Spoon large dollops of the horseradish cream in and around the salad.

Sprinkle the lemon juice over the top and drizzle generously with olive oil. Sprinkle with sea salt and freshly ground black pepper.

Scatter the dill over the top and serve.

# RAW CAULIFLOWER 'TABOULEH' PACKED WITH FRAGRANT HERBS

½ cauliflower, roughly
   broken into pieces
2 garlic cloves, peeled
1 large handful of basil
   leaves
1 large handful of flat-leaf
   (Italian) parsley
1 large handful of mint
   leaves
75 g (2½ oz/½ cup) roughly
   chopped sun-dried
   tomatoes
juice of 1 lemon
a good glug of extra virgin
   olive oil

*Full of refreshing, bright flavours, this raw, zingy salad has a lovely blend of textures. The sun-dried tomatoes add a rich, sweet flavour burst. This salad is fantastic on its own as a light lunch, or great served as a side dish.*

**SERVES 2** as a light lunch, or **4** as a side ❖ GF, DF, VEG, V

Put the cauliflower and garlic in a food processor. Pulse a couple of times, until the texture is similar to rice. Add the basil, parsley and mint, then pulse a few more times, until well combined.

Transfer to a mixing bowl and add the sun-dried tomatoes, lemon juice, olive oil and a generous pinch of sea salt and freshly ground black pepper.

Toss well and serve.

# BRAISED LENTILS IN A RICH TOMATO AND PRESERVED LEMON SAUCE

2 tablespoons ghee, butter
   or olive oil
1 brown onion, diced
4 garlic cloves, roughly
   chopped
1 large handful of thyme
   leaves, roughly chopped
2 tablespoons thinly
   sliced Preserved lemon
   (page 221)
400 g (14 oz) tin lentils,
   or 270 g (9½ oz/1¼ cups)
   cooked lentils, drained
2 x 400 g (14 oz) tins
   chopped tomatoes
1 large handful of basil
   leaves, roughly torn or
   chopped
grated parmesan cheese,
   to serve
extra virgin olive oil, for
   drizzling

*Fresh herbs add a lovely fragrant undertone to this simple yet deeply tasty lentil dish, enhancing the richness of the tomato sauce, which is also lifted by a subtle preserved lemon kick. The lentils are lovely as a light meal, or served alongside meat or fish.*

**SERVES 2** as a light meal, or **4** as a side ❀ GF, DF (if no ghee or cheese used), VEG, V (if no ghee, butter or cheese used)

Melt the ghee in a large saucepan over medium heat. Add the onion, garlic and thyme and cook, stirring regularly, for 10 minutes, or until the onion is soft and slightly browned.

Add the preserved lemon, lentils and tomatoes and bring to a gentle simmer. Cook for a further 20 minutes, or until the tomatoes are thick and pulpy.

Stir in most of the basil, reserving some for serving. Season generously with sea salt and freshly ground black pepper.

Serve scattered with the parmesan and reserved basil, and a drizzle of olive oil.

# GARLIC AND LEMON ZEST PEAS SMASHED WITH AVOCADO

*Zingy, light and crunchy, this zesty salad has a creamy texture from the avocado, and a lovely garlic hum. Splendid on its own as a light lunch, it also complements most types of meat or fish.*

**SERVES 2** ❖ GF, DF (if no ghee or butter used), VEG, V (if no ghee or butter used)

2 tablespoons ghee, butter or olive oil
4 garlic cloves, finely chopped
1 brown onion, thinly sliced
420 g (15 oz/3 cups) frozen or shelled fresh peas
zest and juice of 1 lemon
1 handful of flat-leaf (Italian) parsley, chopped
flesh of 1 avocado, roughly chopped
40 g (1½ oz/¼ cup) pepitas (pumpkin seeds)
extra virgin olive oil, to serve

Melt the ghee in a large saucepan over medium heat, until sizzling. Add the garlic, onion and peas and cook, stirring regularly, for a couple of minutes, until the garlic and onion start to soften and brown.

Add the lemon zest and juice, parsley, avocado, pepitas and a large pinch of sea salt and freshly ground black pepper.

Using a fork or potato masher, roughly mash together until well combined. Drizzle with a good glug of olive oil and serve.

# SAGE AND LEMON BUTTERBEANS

*This light lunch or side dish ticks all the boxes for me. It has lovely flavours and textures, tastes beautiful, always leaves me feeling very satisfied — and takes only a few minutes to prepare!*

2 tablespoons ghee, butter or olive oil
1 red onion, diced
3 garlic cloves, roughly chopped
1 large handful of sage
400 g (14 oz) tin butterbeans, drained, or 250 g (9 oz/ 1¼ cups) cooked butterbeans
juice of 1 lemon
extra virgin olive oil, to serve (optional)

**SERVES 1** as a light lunch, or **4** as a side ❖ GF, DF (if no ghee or butter used), VEG, V (if no ghee or butter used)

Melt the ghee in a large frying pan over medium heat. Add the onion, garlic and sage and cook, stirring, for 10 minutes, or until the onion is browned and slightly crispy. Add the beans and continue to cook for a minute or so.

Add the lemon juice and a good pinch of sea salt and freshly ground black pepper. Cook for a further 2–3 minutes, just to let all the flavours sink into each other.

Remove from the heat and add a little more seasoning if needed. Serve immediately, drizzled with a good glug of olive oil if you like.

# CARAMELISED PUMPKIN WITH PARSLEY AND BLACK OLIVE GREMOLATA

*We enjoy this dish on a hot summer's day, with grilled chicken or fish. The salty, citrusy gremolata gives the sweet, crispy baked pumpkin a refreshing zing. Although I suggest butternut pumpkin here, this dish works well with most types of pumpkin.*

**SERVES 2** as a light meal, or **4** as a side ❖ GF, DF, VEG, V (if no honey used)

½ butternut pumpkin (squash), cut into wedges about 1 cm (½ inch) thick
2 tablespoons extra virgin olive oil
2 tablespoons honey, or maple or agave syrup
3 large handfuls of flat-leaf (Italian) parsley, roughly chopped
150 g (5½ oz/1 cup) pitted and roughly chopped black olives
zest and juice of 1 lemon

Preheat the oven to 180°C (350°F/Gas 4).

Lay the pumpkin on a baking tray and drizzle with the olive oil and honey. Sprinkle generously with sea salt and freshly ground black pepper. Bake for 30 minutes, or until tender, golden and caramelised.

When the pumpkin is nearly ready, make a gremolata by combining the parsley, olives, lemon zest and lemon juice in a bowl. Mix together well.

Serve the pumpkin warm, sprinkled with the gremolata.

# COLOURFUL ROASTED VEGETABLE MEDLEY

6-8 yams, ends trimmed
½ butternut pumpkin
 (squash), peeled and
 cut into wedges
¼ red cabbage, roughly
 sliced
2 carrots, peeled and roughly
 chopped
1 fennel bulb, tough outer
 layer discarded, inner part
 roughly chopped
1 garlic bulb, cloves peeled
 and lightly smashed
1 large handful of fresh
 herbs, such as basil, thyme
 and parsley
extra virgin olive oil, for
 drizzling
juice of 1 lemon

*Sometimes I just crave a beautiful selection of roasted vegetables — sweet, tender, crisp-edged and full of flavour. This humble dish is perfect for a simple dinner paired with grilled steak, chicken or fish, or can even be enjoyed on its own as a light meal. Why not get as creative as possible, and incorporate as many new and exciting seasonal coloured vegetables as you can?*

**SERVES 4** as a side ❖ GF, DF, VEG, V

Preheat the oven to 180°C (350°F/Gas 4).

Arrange the vegetables and garlic in a large baking dish. Sprinkle with the herbs. Drizzle with olive oil, then squeeze the lemon juice over the top. Season generously with sea salt and freshly ground black pepper.

Bake for 40–45 minutes, or until the vegetables are well roasted, tender inside and crispy on the outside.

# ROASTED LETTUCE HEARTS WITH LEMON ZEST AND GARLIC AÏOLI

*I absolutely adore this dish. Roasting the lettuce gives it the most wonderful sweetness and a silky yet crunchy texture — an exciting new way to enjoy salad greens. Serve it as simply as possible, with a drizzle of aïoli, allowing the subtle flavours of the lettuce to shine through.*

**SERVES 4** as a side ❖ GF, DF, VEG

3–4 baby cos (romaine) lettuces
extra virgin olive oil, for drizzling
Lemon zest and garlic aïoli (page 216), to serve

Preheat the oven to 180°C (350°F/Gas 4).

To prepare the lettuces, remove the dark outer leaves. Slice each lettuce down the middle lengthways, then lay them in a roasting tin, cut side up. Drizzle with olive oil and sprinkle with sea salt and freshly ground black pepper.

Bake for 25–30 minutes, or until crispy on the edges.

Serve immediately, drizzled with aïoli.

# SLOW-COOKED ZUCCHINI WITH BASIL AND LEMON

*Slowly braising the zucchini in its own liquid and a glug of extra virgin olive oil gives an amazing melt-in-your-mouth texture. Adding lots of basil and a bit of lemon juice right at the end adds a bright burst of freshness.*

*This dish is delicious with fish, quinoa or rice.*

**SERVES 3–4** as a side ❖ GF, DF, VEG, V

extra virgin olive oil, for
   pan-frying
6 zucchini (courgettes),
   sliced into rounds
juice of 1 lemon
2–3 large handfuls of basil
   leaves, roughly chopped

Add enough olive oil to a medium-sized cast-iron saucepan or large heavy-based frying pan to cover the bottom of the pan. Warm the oil over medium heat.

Add the zucchini and stir to coat in the oil. Cover the pan, then reduce the heat to very low. Cook for 20–25 minutes, stirring every few minutes, until the zucchini softens.

Remove from the heat and add the lemon juice, basil and a good pinch of sea salt and freshly ground black pepper.

Stir until combined, then serve.

# LEEK AND CAULIFLOWER GRATIN WITH CRUNCHY HAZELNUTS AND THYME

*Perfect for a cold winter's evening, this gratin is incredibly comforting — just as it should be! This version is topped with crunchy crushed hazelnuts and parmesan cheese, although a sharp cheddar cheese would also work well. A truly warming dish for the soul.*

**SERVES 4** as a side ❖ GF, VEG

½ cauliflower, broken
  into florets
1 leek, white part only, cut
  in half lengthways, then
  roughly chopped
4 garlic cloves, roughly
  chopped
100 g (3½ oz/1 cup) finely
  grated parmesan cheese
750 ml (26 fl oz/3 cups) milk
35 g (1¼ oz/¼ cup) roughly
  chopped hazelnuts
1 handful of thyme leaves

Preheat the oven to 180°C (350°F/Gas 4).

Put the cauliflower, leek, garlic and half the parmesan in a large baking dish. Cover with the milk and season generously with sea salt and freshly ground black pepper.

Sprinkle the remaining parmesan over the top, along with the hazelnuts and thyme.

Bake for 45 minutes, or until the gratin is bubbling around the edges. The vegetables should be tender and cooked through.

Serve hot.

# CHARRED MUSHROOMS WITH BLACK PEPPER AND CREAM

*Try these delectable mushrooms as a side with eggs for breakfast, on buckwheat toast for lunch, or alongside a delicious organic steak for dinner. I like to mix it up a little and experiment with different types of mushrooms, but you can just use portobello mushrooms if you are unable to get your hands on anything fancier.*

*Any dark leaf greens work well here; instead of cavolo nero, try kale, spinach or silverbeet (Swiss chard).*

**SERVES 3–4** as a side ❖ GF, VEG

2 tablespoons ghee, butter
  or olive oil
270 g (9½ oz/3 cups)
  chopped mushrooms
2 handfuls of roughly
  chopped cavolo nero
juice of ½ lemon
125 ml (4 fl oz/½ cup) thin
  (pouring) cream

Melt the ghee in a large frying pan over medium heat. Add the mushrooms and cook for 10–15 minutes, stirring occasionally, until softened and slightly charred.

Add the cavolo nero and cook for another minute, or until wilted. Stir in the lemon juice, cream, a pinch of sea salt and a generous sprinkling of freshly ground black pepper.

Serve immediately.

# ROASTED ONIONS WITH GORGONZOLA AND ROSEMARY

*These fragrant onions are roasted until deliciously tender and sweet with the help of a little honey. The rosemary adds an earthy note, with the blue cheese contributing a strong salty bite to each mouthful.*

*These onions are also good served with crackers as a starter.*

**SERVES 4** as a side ❖ GF, VEG

4 brown onions
2 tablespoons honey, or
  maple or agave syrup
60 ml (2 fl oz/¼ cup) extra
  virgin olive oil
2 rosemary sprigs
crumbled gorgonzola or
  blue vein cheese, to serve

Preheat the oven to 180°C (350°F/Gas 4).

Trim the base and top of the onions, leaving the skin on. Cut the onions as if you are going to cut them in half down the middle, starting from the top, but do not cut all the way down — keep the onions attached at the base.

Make another cut in a similar manner, at a 90-degree angle to the first cut, so the onions are now quartered, but still attached at the base.

Place the onions in a baking dish and drizzle with the honey and olive oil. Sprinkle generously with sea salt and freshly ground black pepper and add the rosemary sprigs.

Roast for 1 hour, or until tender and slightly caramelised.

Serve warm, sprinkled with crumbled cheese.

# HONEYED BALSAMIC SHALLOTS WITH RAISINS

*I have always had a huge love for shallots, and adore using them in many different ways. When cooked right, they are so tender, sweet and full of beautiful flavour. Here they are cooked with balsamic vinegar, thyme and raisins — a delicious combination.*

*I like to serve this dish with poached eggs and buckwheat toast for Sunday brunch.*

**SERVES 3–4** as a side ❖ GF, DF (if no ghee or butter used), VEG, V (if no ghee, butter or honey used)

2 tablespoons ghee, butter or olive oil
10–12 French shallots, peeled
1 handful of thyme leaves, roughly chopped, plus extra to garnish
1 tablespoon honey, or maple or agave syrup
85 g (3 oz/½ cup) raisins
splash of balsamic vinegar
extra virgin olive oil, for drizzling

Melt the ghee in a large frying pan or saucepan over medium heat. Add the shallots, thyme and a pinch of sea salt and freshly ground black pepper. Cook for 10–15 minutes, until the shallots have softened.

Add the honey and raisins and a splash of balsamic vinegar. Cook for a further 5 minutes, or until the shallots are lovely and caramelised.

Serve warm, garnished with extra thyme and drizzled with a little olive oil.

# BEST GRILLED FENNEL IN A SMOKY PAPRIKA TOMATO SAUCE WITH BACON

*I love the subtle undertone of aniseed in this dish, from the aromatic fennel. It harmonises beautifully with the smoky paprika, the tomato, and the saltiness of the bacon.*

*This dish is fabulous served with a beautifully dressed green salad. It is also delicious without bacon, for your vegan or vegetarian friends.*

**SERVES 2** as a light meal, or **4** as a side ❖ GF, DF

400 g (14 oz) tin chopped
   tomatoes
2 tablespoons smoked
   paprika
zest and juice of 1 lemon
2 fennel bulbs, fronds
   reserved, tough outer layer
   discarded, and the inner
   part roughly chopped
4 free-range bacon rashers
extra virgin olive oil, for
   drizzling

Preheat the oven to 180°C (350°F/Gas 4).

Put the tomatoes, paprika, lemon zest and lemon juice in a mixing bowl. Add a pinch of sea salt and freshly ground black pepper and mix well.

Arrange the fennel in a baking dish, then pour the tomato mixture in and around the fennel. Lay the bacon rashers on top and drizzle with olive oil.

Bake for 30 minutes, or until the sauce is bubbling around the edges, and the fennel is cooked through.

Serve garnished with the reserved fennel fronds.

# MAINS

Fantastically delicious and brimming with goodness, these wonderful meals will fill you with simple yet incredible flavours and will nourish you from the inside out. Whether you are looking for a birthday dinner, a casual mid-week meal or you have guests coming over for a fancy feed, I'm sure you'll find something suitable to grace your dinner table.

# HONEY, LEMON AND LAVENDER CHICKEN

*This aromatic roast chicken is deliciously sticky and sweet, with a lovely fragrance from the lavender and thyme; the marinade also works beautifully with chicken legs and thighs.*

*This chicken is fabulous served with steamed millet and a crisp green salad.*

SERVES 4 ❖ GF, DF

2 onions, cut into quarters
250 ml (9 fl oz/1 cup) Home-
    made chicken stock
    (page 206)
1 free-range chicken,
    weighing about 1.5 kg
    (3 lb 5 oz)
1 tablespoon finely chopped
    lavender leaves
2 tablespoons thyme leaves

HONEY AND LEMON
MARINADE
juice of 1 lemon
2 tablespoons honey
60 ml (2 fl oz/¼ cup) extra
    virgin olive oil

Preheat the oven to 180°C (350°F/Gas 4).

Spread the onion quarters in a large baking dish or roasting tin. Pour in the stock, then place the chicken on top.

To make the marinade, cut the lemon in half and squeeze the juice into a small bowl, reserving the lemon halves. Stir the honey and olive oil into the lemon juice until well combined.

Drizzle the marinade over the chicken. Place a reserved lemon half in the cavity of the chicken and add the other lemon half to the baking dish. Sprinkle the chicken and onion with the lavender and thyme and season generously with sea salt and freshly ground black pepper.

Bake for 1½ hours, basting the chicken with the marinade and pan juices halfway through cooking. To test if the chicken is cooked, insert a fork or skewer into the thickest part of the thigh — the juices should run clear.

Transfer the chicken to a wooden chopping board and leave to rest for 5 minutes or so before carving.

# GREEN OLIVE, TOMATO AND BASIL ROASTED CHICKEN LEGS

*The flavours in this exquisitely simple dish are truly wonderful. Everything comes together quickly, making it an excellent weeknight choice, but it's also sublime enough to impress company. The chicken is tender and moist, with a subtle sweetness from the basil and cherry tomatoes, and a slight salt tang from the olives.*

*Lovely served over your favourite vegetable mash.*

**SERVES 4** ❖ GF, DF

6–8 free-range chicken
   drumsticks, skin on
90 g (3¼ oz/½ cup) green
   olives
250 g (9 oz) cherry tomatoes
1 large handful of basil
   leaves
a good drizzle of extra virgin
   olive oil
juice of 1 lemon

Preheat the oven to 180°C (350°F/Gas 4).

Arrange the chicken, olives, tomatoes and basil in a large baking dish. Drizzle with olive oil and sprinkle with a large pinch of sea salt and freshly ground black pepper. Squeeze the lemon juice over the top.

Bake for 45 minutes, or until the chicken is lovely and golden, basting with the juices halfway through cooking. To test if the chicken is cooked, insert a fork or skewer into the thickest part of the meat — the juices should run clear.

Serve immediately.

# CAULIFLOWER 'COUSCOUS' TOSSED WITH SALMON AND A FRIED EGG

*Ready in less than half an hour, this perfectly balanced meal uses crumbled and lightly blanched cauliflower to make a delicious and lightly-textured couscous, tossed with rich, buttery salmon, sweet basil and extra virgin olive oil, and then topped with a fried egg.*

**SERVES 2** ❖ GF, DF (if no ghee or butter used)

½ cauliflower, broken
   into florets
1 tablespoon ghee, butter
   or olive oil
2 free-range eggs
1 large handful of basil
   leaves, roughly torn, plus
   extra to garnish
2 salmon fillets, skin on, cut
   into small bite-sized pieces
juice of 1 lemon
a good drizzle of extra virgin
   olive oil

Put the cauliflower in a food processor. Pulse until it has a rice-like consistency, then transfer to a heatproof bowl.

Melt the ghee in a frying pan over medium heat. Crack the eggs into the pan, then cook until the yolks are done to your liking.

While the eggs are cooking, cover the cauliflower with boiling water. Leave to sit for 1 minute, then drain immediately.

Toss the cauliflower in a bowl with the basil, salmon, lemon juice, olive oil and a pinch of sea salt and freshly ground black pepper. The salmon will cook perfectly from the heat of the cauliflower.

Serve each portion topped with a fried egg and garnished with extra basil.

# BROWN BUTTER FISH WITH LEMON AND CAPERS

*I like to use snapper for this quick, simple dish, as the flesh is lovely and delicate. Here it is paired with a stunning brown butter sauce that leaves a nutty rich taste with each mouthful. Basil and parsley are added to the sauce right at the very end, for a subtle touch of sweetness.*

**SERVES 2** ❖ GF (if using gluten-free flour)

3 tablespoons plain
  (all-purpose) flour; use
  buckwheat, brown rice,
  spelt or other flour
  of your choice
2 fish fillets, such as snapper,
  or other delicately textured
  white-fleshed fish
2 tablespoons ghee, butter
  or olive oil

LEMON AND CAPER SAUCE
50 g (1¾ oz) butter
juice of 1 lemon
50 g (1¾ oz/¼ cup) capers
1 handful of basil leaves,
  roughly chopped
1 handful of flat-leaf (Italian)
  parsley, roughly chopped

Put the flour on a large plate. Sprinkle with a large pinch of sea salt and freshly ground black pepper and mix together. Dredge the fish fillets in the flour, so they are evenly coated, shaking off any excess.

Melt the ghee in a large frying pan over medium heat. Cook the fish for 2–3 minutes on each side, until golden and just cooked through.

Place the fish on a warmed plate and cover with foil to keep warm and moist.

Wipe out the pan with paper towel and return to the heat. To make the sauce, add the butter and cook over medium heat for about 5 minutes, or until it starts to turn a lovely dark golden colour and smells beautifully fragrant and nutty. Remove from the heat and add the lemon juice and capers — it's a good idea to stand back as the hot butter may splutter a little.

Add the basil and parsley and then swirl the contents of the pan around. Season with sea salt and freshly ground black pepper.

Return the fish to the pan and spoon the juices on top. Serve immediately.

# LAMB LEG STEAKS WITH MINT AND APPLE CIDER SAUCE

*Sometimes I just crave a juicy, beautifully cooked steak. If you haven't tried lamb steaks before, I would definitely recommend them. When cooked well, they are very rich and tender — and sublime topped with this simple mint, honey and apple cider vinegar sauce.*

**SERVES 2** ❖ GF, DF

2 large organic lamb leg steaks, each weighing about 300 g (10½ oz) and about 2 cm (¾ inch) thick, at room temperature
2–3 tablespoons olive oil

MINT AND APPLE CIDER SAUCE
60 ml (2 fl oz/¼ cup) apple cider vinegar
2 tablespoons honey, or maple or agave syrup
1 large handful of mint leaves

Sprinkle the steaks with a good pinch of sea salt and freshly ground black pepper, then rub on both sides with the olive oil. Set aside.

To make the sauce, put the vinegar and honey in a small saucepan over low heat and bring to a gentle boil. Remove from the heat, then add the mint and a pinch of sea salt and freshly ground black pepper. Stir well, then cover with a lid — this helps the flavours to really mix together.

Heat a chargrill pan or frying pan over high heat. Cook the lamb for 3 minutes on each side for medium-rare. Leave to rest for 5 minutes.

Carve the lamb and serve drizzled with the sauce.

# APPLE AND SAGE
# PORK CASSOULET

*This delectable winter meal will leave you feeling warm, comforted and satisfied. The rich, creamy slow-cooked pork just melts in your mouth, the sage adds an earthy undertone, and the soft sweetness of the apple shines through perfectly.*

*I love to serve the cassoulet with freshly steamed millet, brown rice or Creamy cauliflower mash (see page 97).*

**SERVES 4** ❖ GF (if using gluten-free flour), DF (if no ghee or butter used)

1 tablespoon ghee, butter or olive oil

6 French shallots, roughly chopped

4 garlic cloves, roughly chopped

1 large handful of sage leaves

500 g (1 lb 2 oz) organic pork shoulder, cut into 2.5 cm (1 inch) cubes

2 tablespoons plain (all-purpose) brown rice flour (see Note)

185 ml (6 fl oz/¾ cup) sweet white wine or apple juice

1 litre (35 fl oz/4 cups) Home-made vegetable stock (page 207) or chicken stock (page 206)

2 carrots, chopped

2 apples, skin on, cored and cut into wedges

175 g (6 oz) frozen or shelled fresh peas

Melt the ghee in a large flameproof casserole dish over medium heat. Add the shallot, garlic and sage and sauté for 10 minutes, or until the shallot is soft and slightly browned.

Add the pork, then sprinkle the flour over. Continue to cook, stirring regularly, for about 10 minutes, until the meat is browned all over.

Stir in the wine, then simmer for about 5 minutes, until it has evaporated.

Add the stock, carrot and apple, then reduce the heat to low. Simmer, uncovered, for 1½ hours, or until the meat is tender and the sauce is lovely and thick, adding a little more stock if needed.

Stir in the peas and cook for a further 5–10 minutes, or until the peas are just tender. Serve hot.

## NOTE ⟫⟫⟫

You could use any flour of your choice — buckwheat, spelt, wholemeal (whole-wheat) and tapioca flour all work well.

# RED WINE, ROSEMARY AND GARLIC BEEF PIE

*A hearty, nourishing version of a family classic, crowned with a crisp, buttery spelt-flour crust.*

*For a gluten-free option, simply replace the spelt in the pastry with 195 g (7 oz / 1½ cups) buckwheat flour, or 225 g (8 oz / 1½ cups) brown rice flour.*

**SERVES 4** ❖ GF (if using buckwheat flour or brown rice flour)

## FILLING
2 tablespoons ghee, butter or olive oil
1 brown onion, roughly chopped
1 garlic bulb, cloves peeled and roughly chopped
1 handful of rosemary, finely chopped
1 handful of thyme leaves, roughly chopped
500 g (1 lb 2 oz) minced (ground) organic beef
2 tablespoons plain (all-purpose) wholemeal (whole-wheat) spelt, buckwheat or rice flour
185 ml (6 fl oz/¾ cup) red wine
1 litre (35 fl oz/4 cups) Home-made beef stock (page 206)

## PASTRY
225 g (8 oz/1½ cups) plain wholemeal spelt flour, plus extra for kneading
100 g (3½ oz) cold butter, diced
1 free-range egg
1–2 tablespoons milk or beaten egg, for glazing

To make the pastry, put the flour and butter in a food processor and pulse to a breadcrumb-like texture. Add the egg and 60 ml (2 fl oz/¼ cup) water, then pulse until the dough starts to come together. Transfer to a floured work surface and softly knead until smooth. Dust lightly with flour, cover and rest in the fridge for 30 minutes.

To make the filling, melt the ghee in a large flameproof casserole dish over medium heat. Add the onion, garlic, rosemary and thyme and sauté for 10 minutes, or until the onion is soft and slightly browned. Add the beef and sprinkle the flour over the top. Cook, stirring regularly, for 5 minutes, until the meat is browned all over. Season with sea salt and freshly ground black pepper.

Stir in the wine, reduce the heat to low, then simmer, uncovered, for about 5 minutes, until the wine has evaporated. Stir in the stock and simmer, uncovered, for 30–40 minutes, or until all the liquid has evaporated.

Meanwhile, preheat the oven to 180°C (350°F/Gas 4).

Spoon the filling into a lightly greased pie dish. Roll the pastry out about 1 cm (½ inch) thick and 1 cm (½ inch) larger than your pie dish, then place over the filling. Rustically pinch the pastry edges, prick the top of the pastry a few times with a fork, then glaze with the milk.

Bake for 35–40 minutes, or until golden on top. Leave to rest for 5 minutes before slicing. Serve hot.

# MEATBALLS WITH CREAMY CAULIFLOWER MASH

*To make this simple dinner an absolute winner, be sure to buy really good-quality sausages for the quick and easy meatballs.*

**SERVES 4** ❖ GF, DF (if no ghee, butter, cheese or cream used)

1 cauliflower, broken into florets

8 organic, gluten-free beef, lamb or pork sausages

4 tablespoons ghee, butter or olive oil

2–3 garlic cloves, crushed

1¼–1½ heaped tablespoons dijon mustard

½ teaspoon ground nutmeg

1 handful of grated parmesan cheese (optional)

a dash of thin (pouring) cream (optional)

1 small handful of roughly chopped flat-leaf (Italian) parsley

extra virgin olive oil, for drizzling

Put the cauliflower in a large saucepan and cover with water. Bring to the boil, then reduce the heat and simmer for 10–12 minutes, until very tender.

While the cauliflower is cooking, snip the sausages apart, then squeeze the meat out of the skins, into smaller portions. Using your hands, roll them into evenly sized balls; you should get about four meatballs from each sausage. Melt 2 tablespoons of the ghee in a large frying pan over medium heat. Add the meatballs and cook, turning every so often, for 4–5 minutes, or until golden brown and cooked through. Keep warm.

Strain the cauliflower, then return to the saucepan with the remaining ghee, along with the garlic, mustard, nutmeg, and the parmesan and cream, if using. Season generously with sea salt and freshly ground black pepper, then mash well using a potato masher.

To serve, divide the mash among four plates, then top with the meatballs, a sprinkling of parsley, and a drizzle of olive oil.

# EGGPLANT INVOLTINI

*I can't begin to say how much I love this scrumptious dish. Meat lovers probably won't even notice it is vegetarian!*

SERVES 2–3 as a main meal, or 3–4 as a side ❖ GF, DF (if no ghee or butter used), VEG, V (if no ghee, butter or honey used)

80–125 ml (2½–4 fl oz/
⅓–½ cup) melted ghee,
butter or olive oil
2 eggplants (aubergines),
cut lengthways into slices
about 1 cm (½ inch) thick
1 brown onion, diced
1 tablespoon honey, or maple
or agave syrup
250 ml (9 fl oz/1 cup) Simple
basil and garlic tomato
sauce (page 209)
roughly chopped flat-leaf
(Italian) parsley, to garnish

## CASHEW CHEESE
310 g (11 oz/2 cups) cashew
nuts, soaked in water
overnight, then drained
and rinsed
juice of ½ lemon
1 garlic clove, peeled

Preheat the oven to 180°C (350°F/Gas 4). Grease two baking trays with some of the melted ghee.

Lay the eggplant on the baking trays. Drizzle with 2–4 tablespoons of the melted ghee, then sprinkle with sea salt and freshly ground black pepper. Bake for 25–30 minutes, or until soft and lightly golden. Remove from the oven and leave to cool; leave the oven on.

Meanwhile, heat another 2 tablespoons of ghee in a large frying pan over medium heat. Add the onion and sauté for 10 minutes, or until soft. Drizzle with the honey, then add 2 tablespoons water. Reduce the heat to low and cook for a further 15–20 minutes, until the onion becomes caramelised and golden. Remove from the heat and leave until cool enough to handle.

To make the cashew cheese, put the cashews in a food processor with the lemon juice, garlic and a pinch of sea salt and black pepper. Blend until smooth.

Mix the onion and cashew cheese in a large bowl until well combined. Spoon 2 tablespoons of the filling onto the middle of each eggplant slice. Roll each piece tightly and place in a lightly greased baking dish. Spoon the tomato sauce over the top. Bake for 25–30 minutes.

Cool for 5 minutes, garnish with parsley and serve.

# SPANISH BRAISED CHICKPEAS

*Lemon adds a good citrus kick to these smoky, hearty chickpeas. When I'm feeling a little fancy, I like to add some grilled chorizo sausage for a truly wonderful combination.*

*For vegans and vegetarians, serve the chickpeas with steamed rice or millet to round out the plant protein.*

**SERVES 2** ❈ GF, DF (if no ghee or butter used), VEG, V (if no ghee or butter used)

3 tablespoons ghee, butter or olive oil

5 French shallots, roughly chopped

3 teaspoons smoked paprika

400 g (14 oz) tin chickpeas, drained, or 250 g (9 oz/ 1¼ cups) cooked chickpeas

2 x 400 g (14 oz) tins chopped tomatoes

juice of 1 lemon

1 large handful of basil leaves, roughly chopped

Melt the ghee in a flameproof casserole dish over medium heat. Add the shallot and paprika and cook, stirring, for 10 minutes, or until the shallot is soft and slightly browned.

Add the chickpeas, tomatoes and a large pinch of sea salt and freshly ground black pepper. Mix together well, then simmer, uncovered, over low heat for about 30 minutes, or until the sauce is thick and pulpy.

Add the lemon juice and most of the basil and stir well. Serve garnished with the remaining basil.

# MILLET PILAFF WITH GRAPES, FETA, MINT AND CUCUMBER

*Millet is an ancient seed that is rich in iron, vitamins and calcium, and is naturally gluten free. It is relatively quick to cook and has a lovely light texture. The trick is to cook the millet in a delicious home-made stock for a wonderful depth of flavour.*

*With its blend of sweet, salty and fresh flavours, this pilaff is the perfect meal for a warm summer's evening. It can be made in advance and served cold.*

**SERVES 4** ❈ GF, VEG (if vegetable stock used)

225 g (8 oz/1 cup) raw hulled millet

500 ml (17 fl oz/2 cups) Home-made chicken stock (page 206) or vegetable stock (page 207)

1 handful of red or green grapes

100 g (3½ oz) feta cheese, crumbled or diced

1 large handful of mint leaves, roughly chopped

½ cucumber, sliced lengthways, then cut into pieces 1 cm (½ inch) thick

50 g (1¾ oz/¼ cup) capers

juice of 1 lemon

60 ml (2 fl oz/¼ cup) extra virgin olive oil

Put the millet, stock and a pinch of sea salt in a large saucepan. Bring to a gentle boil over medium heat, then reduce the heat slightly and simmer, covered, for 15 minutes, or until the grains absorb almost all of the stock. Stir once or twice during cooking, but be careful not to overmix, as this will break up the texture of the grains.

Remove from the heat and leave to sit, covered, for 10 minutes.

Fluff up the millet grains with a fork. Transfer to a bowl, then add the remaining ingredients and a good pinch of sea salt and freshly ground black pepper. Mix gently until combined, then serve.

This dish is equally delicious served hot or cold.

# BEETROOT AND BROWN RICE RISOTTO

*With its beautifully shocking red colour, this dish will brighten up any winter table. Using brown rice means this dish takes longer to cook than your average risotto, but it is well worth the wait, as it is so nourishing. This rich, creamy risotto has a deep earthiness from the beetroot, and is delicious with a generous sprinkling of aged parmesan cheese.*

SERVES 4 ❖ GF, VEG

4 tablespoons butter, ghee or olive oil
1 brown onion, roughly chopped
4 garlic cloves, roughly chopped
220 g (7¾ oz/1 cup) medium-grain brown rice
500 g (1 lb 2 oz) beetroot (beets), peeled and grated
750 ml (26 fl oz/3 cups) Home-made vegetable stock (page 207)
80 g (2¾ oz/¾ cup) finely grated parmesan cheese
thyme leaves, to garnish

Melt 2 tablespoons of the ghee in a large saucepan or flameproof casserole dish over medium heat. Add the onion and garlic and cook, stirring occasionally, for 10 minutes, or until the onion is soft and slightly browned.

Add the rice and cook, stirring gently, for 5 minutes, or until the grains are toasted and fragrant.

Reduce the heat to low, then add the beetroot, stock, and 500 ml (17 fl oz/2 cups) water. Simmer, uncovered, for about 45 minutes, until almost all of the liquid has been absorbed.

Stir in the remaining ghee and half the parmesan. Add a large pinch of sea salt and freshly ground black pepper to taste.

Divide the risotto among four bowls. Serve warm, sprinkled with thyme and the remaining parmesan.

# NUT FLOUR CREPES WITH RICOTTA, WILTED GREENS AND TOASTED SEEDS

*These crepes have a lovely texture and are fantastic for a simple weekend lunch. For a dairy-free version, use Cashew cheese (page 98), or Cashew cream aïoli (page 109) instead of the ricotta.*

**SERVES 3–4;** makes about 5 crepes ❖ GF, VEG

75 g (2½ oz/½ cup) seeds;
I use a mixture of pepitas (pumpkin seeds) and sesame seeds
2 tablespoons ghee, butter or olive oil, plus extra for greasing
2 handfuls of roughly chopped leafy greens, such as spinach, silverbeet (Swiss chard), kale or cavolo nero (remove the stalks before chopping)
115 g (4 oz/½ cup) ricotta cheese

NUT FLOUR CREPES
50 g (1¾ oz/½ cup) almond meal, or other ground nuts
4 large free-range eggs

Toast the seeds in a large dry frying pan over medium heat for about 3 minutes, or until fragrant. Set aside to cool.

To make the crepes, put the almond meal, eggs and a pinch of sea salt in a blender or food processor. Blend until smooth.

Grease a large frying pan and place over high heat. Reduce the heat to low, then add 80 ml (2½ fl oz/⅓ cup) of the crepe batter to the pan, swirling the pan to coat the base. Cook for 1–2 minutes on each side, or until golden.

Repeat with the remaining batter, keeping the stack of cooked crepes warm.

Melt the 2 tablespoons of ghee in a small saucepan over medium heat. Rinse the greens under running water, then add them to the saucepan with only the water clinging to the leaves. Cook, stirring, for a few minutes, or until wilted. Season with sea salt and freshly ground black pepper.

To serve, fill the crepes with the wilted greens, ricotta and toasted seeds. Serve warm.

melted ghee, butter or olive
    oil, for greasing
2 large handfuls of mizuna or
    rocket (arugula), to serve
1 red apple, cored and sliced
    into thin wedges

BURGERS

2 tablespoons ghee, butter
    or olive oil
1 brown onion, chopped
4 garlic cloves, chopped
1 large handful of mixed
    thyme, rosemary and sage,
    finely chopped
180 g (6 oz/2 cups) thinly
    sliced portobello
    mushrooms
215 g (7½ oz/1 cup) cooked
    lentils
200 g (7 oz/2 cups) almond
    meal, or other ground nuts
2 tablespoons dijon mustard
2 free-range eggs

CASHEW CREAM AÏOLI

235 g (8½ oz/1½ cups)
    cashew nuts, soaked in
    water overnight
1 tablespoon dijon mustard
60 ml (2 fl oz/¼ cup) extra
    virgin olive oil
juice of ½ lemon
1 garlic clove
1 teaspoon apple cider
    vinegar

# PORTOBELLO MUSHROOM AND LENTIL BURGERS

*These fantastic vegetarian burgers are full of herbs and garlic, giving them plenty of punch. The protein-packed lentils ensure they are also perfectly filling. To serve, layer the burgers with rocket, then drizzle with the luxurious creamy cashew sauce. No bread buns needed!*

**SERVES 4** ❖ GF, DF (if no ghee or butter used), VEG

To make the cashew cream aïoli, drain the cashews, then rinse well. Place in a food processor with the remaining aïoli ingredients, 125 ml (4 fl oz/½ cup) water and a large pinch of sea salt and freshly ground black pepper. Blend until smooth, thick and creamy, adding a little more water if needed to achieve the perfect consistency. Set aside.

To make the burgers, melt the ghee in a large frying pan over medium heat. Add the onion, garlic and herbs and sauté for 10 minutes, or until the onion is soft and slightly browned. Add the mushrooms and continue to cook for 5 minutes, or until browned. Season generously with sea salt and freshly ground black pepper, remove from the heat and leave to cool.

Put the cooled mushroom mixture in a food processor with the remaining burger ingredients. Blend until well combined.

Grease a large frying pan and place over medium heat.

Shape the mushroom mixture into 12 balls. Place half the balls in the frying pan and press down gently to form burger shapes. Cook for 5–6 minutes on each side, or until lovely and golden. Remove from the pan and keep warm while cooking the remaining burgers.

To serve, stack three burgers per serve with the mizuna, apple wedges and cashew cream aïoli. Sprinkle with extra black pepper and serve.

¼ cabbage (red, white or green), thinly sliced
2 carrots, thinly sliced
1 fennel bulb, fronds reserved, tough outer layer discarded, and the inner part thinly sliced
4–6 radishes, thinly sliced
1 apple, skin left on, grated
1 large handful of mint leaves, roughly torn
1 large handful of basil leaves, roughly torn
400 g (14 oz) tin lentils, drained, or 270 g (9½ oz/ 1¼ cups) cooked lentils
a good drizzle of Best mustard vinaigrette (page 211), to serve

# FENNEL, APPLE AND LENTILS TOSSED WITH MUSTARD VINAIGRETTE

*This dish is definitely a favourite in our household. It really is lip-smackingly tasty and totally addictive, with the sweetness of the apple, the subtle aniseed flavour from the raw fennel, and let's not forget the punchiness of the vinaigrette. Give it a go: I guarantee you will not be disappointed.*

**SERVES 2** ❖ GF, DF, VEG, V (if no worcestershire sauce used in the vinaigrette)

Put the vegetables, apple, herbs and lentils in a large bowl. Pour the vinaigrette over and toss until all the ingredients are well coated.

Transfer to a large platter and serve.

# DESSERTS

Whatever the time of year, a beautifully decadent dessert is the perfect way to end a wonderful meal. The offerings in this chapter have become family favourites, made over and over again with slight variations depending on the season.

During the warmer months we have sweet stone fruits and summer berries, which taste wonderfully tender and sweet in my almond crumble. When the colder season is upon us, I love to use warming spices and rich dark flavours for truly comforting and heavenly desserts.

# BAKED APPLES TOPPED WITH MASCARPONE AND PISTACHIOS

*Topped with creamy mascarpone cheese and salty pistachio nuts, these sticky, sweet, subtly spiced apples are devouringly tender, and always a winner with dinner guests.*

**SERVES 4** ❖ GF, VEG

4 small apples, sliced in half horizontally and cored
2 tablespoons honey, or maple or agave syrup
2 teaspoons ground cinnamon
120 g (4¼ oz/½ cup) mascarpone cheese
40 g (1½ oz/½ cup) raw crushed pistachio nuts

Preheat the oven to 180°C (350°F/Gas 4). Line eight holes of a 12-hole standard muffin tin with baking paper or paper cases. Place an apple half in each lined muffin hole, cut side up.

Put the honey and cinnamon in a small bowl. Add 2 tablespoons boiling water and mix together. Spoon the syrup evenly over the apples.

Bake for 45 minutes, or until the apples are tender. Leave to cool slightly.

Serve topped with the mascarpone and pistachios.

# BAKED BALSAMIC STRAWBERRIES WITH PINE NUTS AND CASHEW CREAM

*This simple but stunningly beautiful dessert will blow you away, with the acidic note from the balsamic vinegar melting into the delectable sweetness of the honey and fruit.*

*The strawberries are served with lovely cashew cream (which you'll need to prepare ahead by soaking the cashew nuts overnight), but you could also serve it with plain yoghurt or whipped cream.*

**SERVES 4** ❖ GF, DF, VEG, V (if no honey used)

40 g (1½ oz/¼ cup) pine nuts
450 g (1 lb/3 cups) strawberries, hulled
80 ml (2½ fl oz/⅓ cup) good-quality balsamic vinegar
3 tablespoons honey, or maple or agave syrup

CASHEW CREAM
235 g (8½ oz/1½ cups) raw cashew nuts, soaked in water overnight
2 tablespoons honey, or agave or maple syrup
juice of ½ lemon

Preheat the oven to 180°C (350°F/Gas 4).

To make the cashew cream, drain the soaked cashews, then rinse well. Place in a food processor with the honey, lemon juice and 125 ml (4 fl oz/½ cup) water. Blend until smooth, thick and creamy, adding a little more water if needed to achieve the perfect consistency. (The cashew cream will keep in the fridge for a day or two, but is best made on the day of serving.)

Toast the pine nuts in a dry frying pan over medium heat for 2–3 minutes, until fragrant, tossing regularly so they don't burn. Transfer to a bowl and set aside to cool.

In another bowl, toss the strawberries with the vinegar and honey.

Transfer the strawberry mixture to a baking dish and bake for 15 minutes. Turn the strawberries with a wooden spoon, then bake for a further 15 minutes, or until the strawberries are soft and juicy. Remove from the oven and leave to cool for 5 minutes or so.

Divide the strawberries among bowls. Sprinkle with the pine nuts, spoon dollops of the cashew cream on top and serve.

# STRAWBERRY TART WITH A CRISPY ALMOND CRUST

*Strawberry and mint are a heavenly match in this lovely tart, encased in a sweet almond pie crust.*

*If you are feeding a crowd, you can easily double the ingredients to make a larger 25 cm (10 inch) tart.*

**SERVES 2–3** ❖ GF, DF (if no butter or yoghurt used), VEG, V (if no butter, yoghurt or honey used)

2 tablespoons melted extra virgin coconut oil or butter, plus extra for greasing

150 g (5½ oz/1½ cups) almond meal

1 tablespoon honey, or maple or agave syrup, plus extra to serve

8–10 strawberries, thinly sliced

plain yoghurt or Honey whipped coconut cream (page 217), to serve

1 handful of mint leaves

Preheat the oven to 180°C (350°F/Gas 4). Grease a 20 cm (8 inch) loose-based flan (tart) tin with the extra coconut oil or butter.

Put the almond meal, coconut oil and honey in a food processor with 1 tablespoon water. Pulse until the mixture resembles coarse crumbs. Tip into the tart tin, then press the dough evenly into the base and sides.

Bake for 8–10 minutes, or until the tart case is golden brown. Remove from the oven and leave to cool completely.

Once cooled, carefully transfer the tart case to a plate. Cover and refrigerate until required; the tart case can be made a day ahead.

Arrange the sliced strawberries on top, then drizzle with a little extra honey. Spoon the yoghurt over the top and serve scattered with the mint leaves.

# BAKED CINNAMON AND VANILLA CUSTARD

*This silky, creamy dessert is infused with subtle notes of cinnamon and vanilla — but you can easily turn it into a chocolate custard by adding a little unsweetened cocoa powder to the basic mixture.*

*I sometimes serve these custards warm from the oven with poached fruit or fruit compote, but they are also excellent cold, and will keep in the fridge for up to two days.*

**SERVES 4** ❖ GF, DF (if no dairy milk used), VEG

375 ml (13 fl oz/1½ cups) full-cream milk or coconut milk
2 tablespoons honey
1½ teaspoons ground cinnamon
1½ teaspoons vanilla extract
2 large free-range eggs

Preheat the oven to 180°C (350°F/Gas 4).

Combine the milk, honey, cinnamon and vanilla in a saucepan. Bring to a gentle boil, stirring to dissolve the honey. Remove from the heat and leave to cool for 10 minutes or so, until cooled to lukewarm.

Crack the eggs into a small bowl and whisk until combined. Gently whisk the eggs into the lukewarm milk mixture until well combined.

Pour the custard into four 150 ml (5 fl oz) ramekins. Place the ramekins in a baking dish, then pour enough hot water into the baking dish to reach halfway up the side of the ramekins.

Bake for 30 minutes, or until slightly golden on top. Serve warm or chilled.

# BLUEBERRY AND ALMOND CRUMBLE

*A luscious fruit crumble is always a crowd pleaser, and this nourishing, wholesome blueberry version is no exception. The fruit is subtly sweetened with a little honey, spiked with lemon juice, then topped with a deliciously crispy coconut and almond crumble.*

*It is lovely served warm or cold, with a good dollop of yoghurt or cream.*

**SERVES 4–6** ❖ GF, DF (if no butter used), VEG, V (if no honey or butter used)

465 g (1 lb ½ oz/3 cups) fresh or frozen blueberries
juice of ½ lemon
4 tablespoons honey, or maple or agave syrup
3 tablespoons extra virgin coconut oil, or butter
185 g (6½ oz/2 cups) Raw shredded coconut, chia and almond cereal (page 24)

Preheat the oven to 170°C (325°F/Gas 3).

Put the blueberries, lemon juice and 250 ml (9 fl oz/1 cup) water in a large saucepan. Stir in 2 tablespoons of the honey.

Bring to a gentle boil, then reduce the heat and simmer, uncovered, for 15–20 minutes, or until thick and pulpy. Carefully pour the mixture into a baking dish.

Melt the coconut oil and remaining honey together in a small saucepan over low heat. Add the breakfast cereal and mix well to combine. Spoon the mixture over the blueberry filling, then even out with a spoon.

Bake for 15–20 minutes, or until the crumble is golden on top and bubbling around the edges.

# CARAMEL ESPRESSO CREAM POTS LAYERED WITH TOASTED PECAN CRUMBS

*I absolutely adore the combination of textures and balance of flavours in these heavenly little pots. Serving them in individual glasses adds a certain elegance, perfect when you have dinner guests.*

*The separate layers can be prepared a day ahead, but are best assembled on the day of serving for a cleaner look.*

**SERVES 4** ❖ GF, DF (if no dairy cream used), VEG,
V (if no honey or dairy cream used)

125 ml (4 fl oz/½ cup) strong brewed black coffee

3 tablespoons honey, or maple or agave syrup

100 g (3½ oz/1 cup) raw pecans

250 ml (9 fl oz/1 cup) thickened (whipping) cream, whipped or Honey whipped coconut cream (page 217)

3 bananas, peeled and sliced into rounds

To make the caramel espresso sauce, put the coffee and honey in a small saucepan over medium heat. Bring to the boil, then reduce the heat and simmer for 5–10 minutes, until thick and syrupy. Leave to cool.

Toast the pecans in a dry frying pan over medium heat for 2–3 minutes, until fragrant, tossing regularly so they don't burn. Remove to a bowl and set aside to cool.

Once cooled, place the pecans in a food processor and pulse to a crumb-like consistency.

Layer 2 tablespoons of pecan crumbs in each 250 ml (9 fl oz/1 cup) serving glass or jar. Drizzle each with 2 tablespoons of the coffee caramel sauce, top with a layer of whipped cream, then top with enough banana slices to cover the cream.

Repeat the layers. Sprinkle with the remaining pecan crumbs, and drizzle with the remaining coffee caramel sauce.

Served chilled.

# JAM-TOPPED COCONUT YOGHURT PANNA COTTA

*The flavours in this deliciously light, luxuriously silky panna cotta are subtle, but work so well together. The lovely tartness of the yoghurt is rounded out by the natural sweetness of the honey, balancing the coconut nuttiness.*

**SERVES 4** ❖ GF, VEG

Lightly grease four 200 ml (7 fl oz) moulds or glasses, or a 700–800 ml (24–28 fl oz) cake tin with coconut oil. (If using a cake tin, make sure it is not a loose-based one. If the panna cotta are to be enjoyed straight from the dish, you can leave out the greasing.)

Heat the coconut cream in a saucepan over medium heat until slightly steaming, but do not allow to boil. Remove from the heat. Whisk in the agar agar and honey until dissolved, then leave to cool for 5 minutes.

Slowly whisk in the yoghurt, then pour the mixture into the prepared cake tin or moulds.

Leave to set in the fridge overnight, or for at least 4 hours.

To remove the panna cotta from the cake tin or moulds, pour 2 cm (¾ inch) boiling water into a larger baking dish, dip the cake tin or moulds in it for 10 seconds, then carefully invert the panna cotta onto a flat serving plate.

Just before serving, top the panna cotta with the jam and sprinkle with shredded coconut.

This panna cotta can be made a day in advance; cover and refrigerate until required.

melted coconut oil, for greasing (optional)
400 ml (14 fl oz) tin coconut cream
2 tablespoons agar agar flakes
4 tablespoons honey, maple or agave syrup
260 g (9¼ oz/1 cup) plain yoghurt
150 g (5½ oz/½ cup) Raw chia seed berry jam (page 222)
shredded coconut, to serve

# POSH PRUNES IN A SPICED ORANGE SYRUP

*These sweet morsels are delicious spooned over ice cream, plain yoghurt or even your morning porridge. While simmering away, the luscious little prunes soak up all the spicy flavours, which burst in your mouth with every spoonful. Absolutely divine.*

**SERVES 4** ❖ GF, DF, VEG

1 orange
200 g (7 oz/1 cup) pitted
   unsweetened prunes
1 teaspoon ground
   cinnamon
½ teaspoon ground nutmeg
½ teaspoon ground ginger
2 tablespoons honey

Using a vegetable peeler or sharp knife, peel long strips of zest from the orange peel, ensuring the white pith is left on the orange.

Place the orange zest strips in a small saucepan. Squeeze the juice from the orange and add to the pan with the remaining ingredients.

Add 250 ml (9 fl oz/1 cup) water and bring to the boil over medium heat. Reduce the heat to low and simmer for 30 minutes, or until the liquid has reduced to a thick syrup.

Remove the orange zest strips before serving. The prunes will keep in an airtight container in the fridge for up to 1 week.

# COCONUT CREAM POPSICLES

*My kids absolutely love these wholesome popsicles. Free of dairy and refined sugar, these frozen treats are wonderfully creamy, and sweetened lightly with banana and honey.*

*This recipe is very simple and can be easily adapted. Feel free to add whatever tickles your fancy. Fresh berries, shredded coconut and lemon zest, crushed nuts or cocoa nibs are all wonderful additions (see Note). Or get creative and simply let your tastebuds guide you.*

MAKES 12 POPSICLES ❖ GF, DF, VEG, V (if no honey used)

400 ml (14 fl oz) tin coconut cream
1 ripe banana, peeled
2 tablespoons honey, or maple or agave syrup
1 teaspoon vanilla extract

Put the coconut cream, banana, honey and vanilla in a blender or food processor and blend until smooth.

Add any extra flavour ingredients of your choice (see Note), then pulse until just combined.

Pour the mixture into 12 popsicle (ice block/ice lolly) moulds, then insert a wooden popsicle stick into each. Freeze for at least 5 hours or overnight, to set the mixture.

To unmould the popsicles, dip the frozen moulds into a bowl of warm water for about 10 seconds. Give them a little tug every couple of seconds to see if they're loose enough to lift out.

To store the popsicles, remove them from their moulds, wrap each one individually in baking paper, then stack in an airtight freezer-proof container. The popsicles can be frozen for up to 2 weeks.

NOTE
Here are some extra flavour combinations to experiment with. Chocolate: add 30 g (1 oz/¼ cup) drinking cocoa or unsweetened cocoa powder; for chocolate chip, add 30 g (1 oz/¼ cup) cocoa nibs. Nut lovers: add 35 g (1¼ oz/¼ cup) crushed nuts. Fruity: add 75 g (2½ oz/½ cup) fresh berries or fruit. Tropical: add the zest of 1 lemon, plus 20 g (¾ oz/¼ cup) shredded coconut.

# BEETROOT CHOCOLATE PUDDING

*Fluffy and light on the outside, fudgy and molten on the inside, this rich chocolate pudding contains a secret ingredient: beetroot, which adds a lovely moistness. With the addition of hot chocolate sauce, this dessert is best enjoyed in small portions. If you feel the need to offer cream — and well you might! — I recommend a jug of thin (pouring) cream.*

*This pudding can be made in one large baking dish, or in four smaller ramekins.*

**SERVES 4** ❖ GF, DF (if no butter used), VEG

## PUDDING
280 g (10 oz/2 cups firmly packed) peeled and grated beetroot (beet)
4 free-range eggs
75 g (2½ oz/⅔ cup) good-quality unsweetened cocoa powder
6 tablespoons honey, or maple or agave syrup
1 tablespoon apple cider vinegar
1 teaspoon bicarbonate of soda (baking soda)

## CHOCOLATE SAUCE
3 tablespoons extra virgin coconut oil, or unsalted butter
2 tablespoons honey
2 tablespoons good-quality unsweetened cocoa powder
1 teaspoon vanilla extract

Preheat the oven to 180°C (350°F/Gas 4).

Put all the pudding ingredients in a large bowl. Using a wooden spoon, mix until very well combined.

Pour the batter into a lightly greased 750 ml (26 fl oz/3 cup) baking dish, or divide among four 250 ml (9 fl oz/1 cup) ramekins. Bake for 20 minutes.

While the pudding is in the oven, make the chocolate sauce. Melt the coconut oil and honey together in a small saucepan over medium heat. Remove from the heat, then whisk in the cocoa and vanilla until well combined.

After the pudding has been baking for 20 minutes, pour the chocolate sauce over the top. Bake for a further 15 minutes, or until the pudding is well risen, but is still slightly soft in the centre.

Best served warm.

# WATERMELON AND RASPBERRY COCONUT GRANITA

*Vibrant and sweet, this icy dessert is full of summer-time flavours – exquisitely refreshing on those hot lazy days. If you've never made a granita before, you'll be amazed how easy it is. Simply mix your ingredients, transfer to trays or dishes and freeze; every hour or so, take the granita out and scrape it up with a fork to form icy crystals.*

*Most types of berries work well in this granita. You can use frozen berries instead of fresh; just thaw them to room temperature before using.*

**SERVES 4** ❖ GF, DF, VEG, V (if no honey used)

300 g (10½ oz/2 cups)
  chopped fresh watermelon
  flesh, at room temperature
250 g (9 oz/2 cups)
  raspberries
250 ml (9 fl oz/1 cup)
  coconut milk
juice of 1 lemon
3 tablespoons honey, or
  maple or agave syrup
shredded coconut, to serve
  (optional)

Put the watermelon and raspberries in a blender or food processor, then purée until smooth. Add the coconut milk, lemon and honey and blend for a further 5 seconds.

Pour the mixture into two 20 cm (8 inch) square baking dishes or deep-sided metal trays, smoothing the mixture out to about 1 cm (½ inch) thick.

Transfer to the freezer, leaving the granita uncovered. Every hour or so, scrape the mixture with a fork to break up the ice crystals and keep the granita light and fluffy. Repeat the scraping process once an hour for 3–4 hours, until you have a soft and snowy granita.

The granita will keep in an airtight container in the freezer for a week or so. To serve, roughly fluff up the crystals again with a fork, spoon into bowls, then sprinkle with coconut if desired.

# PINEAPPLE SALAD WITH COCONUT HONEY SYRUP AND GOAT'S CHEESE

*A drizzle of coconut honey syrup lends a magnificent tropical hint to this summery salad, with goat's cheese adding a deliciously creamy note. I've used fresh thyme in this salad, but mint also tastes divine.*

*Serve warm or cold.*

**SERVES 4** ❈ GF, VEG

½ ripe pineapple, peeled, cored and cut into bite-sized pieces

60 g (2¼ oz/½ cup) crumbled goat's or feta cheese

1 small handful of thyme leaves

2 tablespoons honey, or maple or agave syrup

60 ml (2 fl oz/¼ cup) extra virgin coconut oil

juice of 1 lemon

Arrange the pineapple on a large plate, then scatter the cheese and thyme on top.

Melt the honey and coconut oil together in a small saucepan over medium heat. Remove from the heat and stir in the lemon juice.

Drizzle the syrup over the salad.

Serve immediately, or allow to cool.

# SALTED CHOCOLATE AND ORANGE MOUSSE

*Made entirely with natural, nutrient-rich ingredients, this decadent, creamy mousse satisfies those sweet cravings.*

*If you have a food processor that does not tend to blend well, soak the dates for a few hours before using; this will help the mousse achieve a smoother consistency.*

*Go ahead, indulge — your body will love you for it.*

SERVES 4 ❖ GF, DF, VEG, V

100 ml (3½ fl oz) coconut cream
40 g (1½ oz/⅓ cup) good-quality unsweetened cocoa powder
flesh of 1 ripe avocado, roughly chopped
8–10 medjool dates, pitted
zest and juice of 1 orange
1 teaspoon vanilla extract
shredded coconut, for sprinkling

Pour the coconut cream into a small saucepan and warm ever so slightly. Stir in the cocoa powder and whisk until smooth, then leave to cool.

Put the avocado, dates, orange juice and vanilla in a food processor with a pinch of sea salt. Add the cooled cocoa mixture and blend for 1–2 minutes, until completely smooth.

Spoon into four 150 ml (5 fl oz) dessert cups. Sprinkle with the orange zest and shredded coconut and refrigerate for an hour or so, until well chilled.

The mousse will keep covered in the fridge for up to 2 days; garnish with the orange zest and coconut just before serving.

# YOGHURT, MASCARPONE AND BLACKCURRANT CHEESECAKE

*This gluten-free cheesecake is made with coconut flour. You could use another flour of your choice, but you will need to increase the quantity to 75 g (2½ oz / ½ cup), as coconut flour is very absorbent. Spelt, buckwheat and nut flour all work well.*

**SERVES 8** ❖ GF, VEG

## CHEESECAKE
260 g (9¼ oz/1 cup) plain yoghurt
240 g (8½ oz/1 cup) mascarpone cheese
6 free-range eggs
35 g (1¼ oz/¼ cup) coconut flour
3 tablespoons honey, or maple or agave syrup
juice and zest of 1 lemon
1 teaspoon vanilla extract

## TOPPING
150 g (5½ oz/1 cup) fresh or frozen blackcurrants
2 tablespoons honey, or maple or agave syrup
50 g (1¾ oz/½ cup) flaked almonds

Preheat the oven to 160°C (315°F/Gas 2–3). Grease a 20 cm (8 inch) loose-based cake tin and line with baking paper.

Put all the cheesecake ingredients in a food processor. Add a pinch of sea salt and blend until smooth. Pour into the prepared cake tin and smooth the top. Bake for 45–50 minutes, or until the cheesecake is cooked through and firm.

Meanwhile, prepare the blackcurrant compote. Combine the blackcurrants, honey and 60 ml (2 fl oz/¼ cup) water in a small saucepan. Bring to a gentle boil over medium heat, then reduce the heat and simmer for 10 minutes, or until the blackcurrants look glossy and delicious. Leave to cool completely.

When the cheesecake is ready, remove it from the oven and leave to cool completely. Carefully remove the cheesecake from the tin and transfer to a serving plate.

Just before serving, top with the blackcurrant compote and scatter the almonds over.

The cheesecake will keep in an airtight container in the fridge for 2–3 days.

# DAINTY NIBBLES

This chapter is full of cherished delights, such as pistachio and prune truffles, a lovely rosemary and yoghurt cake, and a beautiful tea-infused raisin and hazelnut cake inspired by my grandmother.

All the recipes use natural sweeteners such as honey or dates, and a range of wholesome and naturally gluten-free flours. A particular favourite is my moist brownie recipe, which has a base of black beans. Using nutritious and wonderfully textured alternatives in place of regular flour or sugar results in a far healthier and more enjoyable treat!

Hints on Healthy Living

## COCONUT APPLE CAKE

6 free-range eggs

250 ml (9 fl oz/1 cup) melted coconut oil or butter

4 tablespoons honey, or maple or agave syrup

1 apple, grated

grated zest of 1 lemon

65 g (2¼ oz/½ cup) coconut flour

90 g (3¼ oz/1 cup) desiccated coconut

2 teaspoons ground cinnamon

1 teaspoon bicarbonate of soda (baking soda)

## CINNAMON CREAM TOPPING

250 ml (9 fl oz/1 cup) thickened (whipping) cream, whipped, or Cashew cream (page 116)

1–2 tablespoons honey, or agave or maple syrup, to taste

1 teaspoon ground cinnamon, plus extra for dusting

20 g (¾ oz/¼ cup) shredded coconut

# SIMPLE COCONUT APPLE CAKE TOPPED WITH CINNAMON CREAM

*This moist cake is made using coconut flour, making it free of nuts, refined sugar, gluten and dairy. It is subtly sweetened with apple and honey, with a gorgeous hint of spicy cinnamon. If you have never baked with coconut flour before, one thing you need to know is that it is full of fibre, making it extremely absorbent. It needs plenty of moisture, otherwise your cake will be dry and horrible! Also, don't be put off by the six eggs used in this recipe — the cake does not taste 'eggy' at all. In fact it tastes incredibly moist, with a fantastic texture.*

**SERVES 8** ❖ GF, DF (if no cream or butter used), VEG

Preheat the oven to 150°C (300°F/Gas 2). Grease a 20 cm (8 inch) cake tin, or line the tin with baking paper.

Put all the cake ingredients in a food processor with a pinch of sea salt. Blend until well combined, then spoon into the cake tin.

Bake for 45 minutes, or until a skewer inserted in the middle of the cake comes out clean. Leave in the tin to cool completely, before turning out onto a plate.

To make the cinnamon cream, put the cream in a bowl, then gently fold the honey and cinnamon through until incorporated.

Gently spoon the creamy icing over the top of the cake, then spread evenly using a knife or the back of a spoon. Dust with a little extra cinnamon, then sprinkle with the shredded coconut.

The cake will keep in an airtight container for 2–3 days. If topped with cashew cream, the cake can be stored in the pantry; if topped with dairy cream, you'll need to keep it in the fridge.

# BLACK BEAN AND DATE CHOCOLATE BROWNIES

*These sweet, fudgy brownies have a slight caramel taste from the dates, and a rich texture. You would never guess they're made out of black beans; lentils and most other types of cooked beans work well also. Be sure to use good-quality cocoa powder in this recipe, as you can really notice the difference.*

**MAKES 9 SLICES** ❖ GF, DF, VEG

380 g (13½ oz/1½ cups) cooked black beans, or 400 g (14 oz) tinned beans
160 g (5½ oz/1 cup) pitted medjool dates
55 g (2 oz/½ cup) good-quality unsweetened cocoa powder
4 free-range eggs
1 tablespoon apple cider vinegar
1 teaspoon bicarbonate of soda (baking soda)

Preheat the oven to 160°C (315°F/Gas 2–3). Grease a 20 x 24 cm (8 x 9½ inch) slice tin, or line the tin with baking paper.

Put all the ingredients in a food processor and blend until smooth. Pour the batter into the slice tin.

Bake for 30 minutes; you want the brownies to be slightly undercooked, so they have a lovely fudgy texture — be careful not to overcook.

Allow the brownies to cool in the tin for 15–20 minutes, before turning out onto a board and cutting into nine portions.

The brownies will keep in an airtight container in a cool dark place for 2–3 days.

## CARROT CAKE

3 free-range eggs

175 g (6 oz/½ cup) honey, or 125 ml (4 fl oz/½ cup) maple or agave syrup

185 ml (6 fl oz/¾ cup) olive oil

200 g (7 oz/2 cups) almond meal

125 g (4½ oz/¾ cup) rice flour, or 100 g (3½ oz/¾ cup) buckwheat flour

155 g (5½ oz/1 cup firmly packed) grated carrots

½ teaspoon ground cardamom

½ teaspoon ground nutmeg

1 teaspoon ground cinnamon

1 teaspoon ground ginger

½ teaspoon ground cloves

1 teaspoon bicarbonate of soda (baking soda)

## MASCARPONE CREAM

240 g (8½ oz/1 cup) mascarpone cheese

grated zest of 1 lemon

2 teaspoons honey, or maple or agave syrup

## TO DECORATE

2 tablespoons pepitas (pumpkin seeds)

2 tablespoons shredded coconut

2 tablespoons sunflower seeds

# SPICED CHAI CARROT CAKE WITH HONEY MASCARPONE CREAM

*The deep yet delicate blend of spices in this cake pairs beautifully with its rustic texture — a heavenly combination. I particularly love making this cake in the colder months — it is so comforting to fill the kitchen with the warm and delicious smell of spice and cake.*

*For a dairy-free version, you could use Honey whipped coconut cream (page 217) instead of mascarpone cheese in the mascarpone cream topping.*

**SERVES 8** ❖ GF, VEG

Preheat the oven to 160°C (315°F/Gas 2–3). Line a 20 cm (8 inch) cake tin with baking paper.

Put all the cake ingredients in a large bowl. Using a wooden spoon, mix until well combined, then carefully pour the batter into the cake tin.

Bake for 45 minutes, or until a skewer inserted in the middle of the cake comes out clean. Leave in the tin to cool completely, before carefully turning out onto a plate.

To make the mascarpone cream, put the mascarpone, lemon zest and honey in a bowl. Using a spoon, mix until well combined.

Gently spoon the mascarpone cream onto the top of the cooled cake and spread out evenly using a knife or the back of a spoon. Sprinkle with the pepitas, shredded coconut and sunflower seeds.

The cake will keep in an airtight container in the fridge for 2–3 days.

# DECADENT RASPBERRY AND COCONUT CHOCOLATE TORTE

*Containing only nutrient-rich ingredients, this torte is deliciously rich and moist textured. It is sweetened with a little honey and raspberries, and has a base of coconut flour, making it free of gluten, dairy and refined sugar. You could also use 100 g (3½ oz / 1 cup) of ground nuts in this recipe instead of the coconut flour.*

*The torte is lovely served with fresh cream, Honey whipped coconut cream (page 217) or plain yoghurt.*

**SERVES 8** ❖ GF, DF (if no butter used), VEG

3 tablespoons extra virgin coconut oil or unsalted butter

4 tablespoons honey, or maple or agave syrup

125 g (4½ oz/1 cup) fresh or frozen raspberries, or other fruit of your choice

5 free-range eggs

65 g (2¼ oz/½ cup) coconut flour

55 g (2 oz/½ cup) good-quality unsweetened cocoa powder

½ teaspoon bicarbonate of soda (baking soda)

icing (confectioners') sugar, for dusting

Preheat the oven to 150°C (300°F/Gas 2). Grease a 20 cm (8 inch) cake tin, or line with baking paper.

Melt the coconut oil and honey together in a small saucepan over low heat. Set aside to cool.

Put the raspberries in a food processor and blend until smooth. Add the remaining ingredients, including the cooled coconut oil mixture. Blend until smooth, then pour the batter into the cake tin.

Bake for 25–30 minutes, or until a skewer inserted in the middle of the torte comes out clean. Leave in the tin to cool completely, before turning out onto a plate and dusting with icing sugar.

The torte will keep in an airtight container in the fridge for 2–3 days.

# MAPLE AND PECAN TART

*I'm in love with this wholesome version of a classic pie. The filling is exceptionally light, creating a beautifully smooth and slightly silky base for the pecans. For maple syrup lovers, nothing could be more delicious — and best of all, it's very easy to prepare.*

**SERVES 8** ❖ GF (if no spelt used), DF (if no butter used), VEG

## PASTRY

65 g (2¼ oz/½ cup) buckwheat flour, or 80 g (2¾ oz/½ cup) rice flour, or 50 g (1¾ oz/½ cup) spelt flour

125 g (4½ oz/¾ cup) rice flour

45 g (1½ oz/¼ cup) tapioca flour or potato flour, or 30 g (1 oz/¼ cup) cornflour (cornstarch)

60 ml (2 fl oz/¼ cup) melted extra virgin coconut oil or unsalted butter

2 tablespoons honey, or maple or agave syrup

1 egg

## FILLING

125 ml (4 fl oz/½ cup) maple syrup

60 g (2¼ oz) unsalted butter, or 60 ml (2 fl oz/¼ cup) extra virgin coconut oil

4 free-range eggs

1 teaspoon vanilla extract

50 g (1¾ oz/½ cup) whole pecans

To make the pastry, put all the flours, the coconut oil and honey in a food processor with a pinch of sea salt. Process for a minute or so, until the mixture resembles breadcrumbs. Add the egg and process until the dough starts to come together into a ball.

Turn the dough out onto a floured work surface, then knead lightly for a few minutes until it has a soft, silky texture. Cover and chill in the fridge for 20 minutes.

Meanwhile, preheat the oven to 180°C (350°F/Gas 4). Grease a 24 cm (9½ inch) flan (tart) tin.

Roll out the dough on a lightly floured work surface, into a large circle about 5 mm (¼ inch) thick. Carefully press the dough into and up the side of the flan tin. Trim the dough around the edge, then prick the base all over with a fork.

Bake for 10–15 minutes, or until the pastry is lightly golden. Remove from the oven and leave in the tin to cool slightly.

To prepare the filling, melt the maple syrup and butter together over medium heat, then remove from the heat and leave to cool slightly. Gradually whisk in the eggs one at a time, working quickly to ensure that the eggs don't scramble. Stir in the vanilla.

Pour the filling into the pastry case, then scatter the pecans evenly over the filling. Bake for 25–30 minutes, until the filling is golden and cooked through.

This tart is best enjoyed warm on the day of baking. It will keep in an airtight container in the fridge for 2–3 days; gently reheat for serving.

# GRANOLA COOKIES

*I absolutely love the subtle sweetness of the dates in these cookies. They are deliciously soft and chewy, with a great texture. I make a batch at least once a week, as they are wonderful for school lunches.*

*This is the most simple and adaptable recipe, so feel free to add some dried cranberries, chia seeds, or whatever other ingredients take your fancy.*

*Any type of nut butter works well in these cookies. As well as peanut butter, I like almond and cashew butter too.*

**MAKES ABOUT 16** ❖ GF, DF, VEG, V

100 g (3½ oz/1 cup) almond meal

140 g (5 oz/½ cup) peanut butter

75 g (2½ oz/½ cup) mixed seeds, such as sesame, sunflower and pepitas (pumpkin seeds)

160 g (5½ oz/1 cup) pitted medjool dates

1½ teaspoons vanilla extract

½ teaspoon bicarbonate of soda (baking soda)

Preheat the oven to 160°C (315°F/Gas 2–3). Line your largest baking tray with baking paper.

Put all the ingredients in a food processor with a pinch of sea salt. Process until a dough-like texture is achieved — this usually takes a couple of minutes, and you may need to scrape down the side of the processor now and then.

Using your hands, form the mixture into small balls and place them on the baking tray. (They can be put quite close together, as these cookies don't spread during baking.) Using a fork or your hands, press down on the balls to flatten them into cookies.

Bake for 12–15 minutes, or until nice and golden on the outside. Leave to cool on the baking tray, then enjoy!

The cookies will keep in an airtight container in a cool dark place for 3–4 days.

# PISTACHIO AND PRUNE TRUFFLES

*I love making these super-simple yet slightly posh chocolatey truffles. Containing only a handful of simple and nourishing ingredients, they are free of refined sugar, gluten and dairy. Just the thing for when you're craving something a little special.*

**MAKES ABOUT 25** ❖ GF, DF, VEG, V

110 g (3¾ oz/¾ cup) raw pistachio nut kernels
105 g (3½ oz/½ cup) pitted prunes
30 g (1 oz/¼ cup) good-quality unsweetened cocoa powder

Put the pistachios in a food processor. Pulse a couple of times, until ground into a dense flour. Transfer 35 g (1¼ oz/¼ cup) of the ground pistachios to a separate bowl and set aside for dusting the truffles.

Add the prunes and cocoa powder to the food processor and blend for 1–2 minutes, or until the mixture starts to come together like a dough.

Using your hands, form the mixture into small balls; you may need to dip your hands in water to stop the mixture sticking.

Roll the balls in the reserved ground pistachios until well coated. Transfer to a plate, then chill the truffles in the fridge for at least 30 minutes to set.

The truffles can be kept at room temperature in an airtight container, but I find they are best kept in the fridge. They will keep for 3–4 days.

# ROSEWATER ALMOND CAKE

*This simple almond cake has delightful undertones of rosewater, complemented nicely with a little lemon zest. A slice of this beautiful cake is perfect when you desire something sweet, moist and comforting.*

**SERVES 8** ❖ GF, DF (if no butter used) , VEG

200 g (7 oz/2 cups) almond meal
3 free-range eggs
4 tablespoons honey, or agave or maple syrup
80 ml (2½ fl oz/⅓ cup) extra virgin coconut oil, or 80 g (2¾ oz) unsalted butter
grated zest of 2 lemons
2 tablespoons rosewater
1 teaspoon bicarbonate of soda (baking soda)
35 g (1¼ oz/⅓ cup) flaked almonds
unsprayed rose petals, for decorating (optional)

Preheat the oven to 160°C (315°F/Gas 2–3). Grease a 20 cm (8 inch) cake tin, or line with baking paper.

Put the almond meal, eggs, honey and coconut oil in a food processor. Add the lemon zest, rosewater and bicarbonate of soda and blend until smooth.

Pour the batter into the cake tin. Scatter the almonds over the top.

Bake for 35–40 minutes, or until a skewer inserted in the middle of the cake comes out clean.

Leave in the tin to cool completely, before turning out onto a plate. Garnish with a sprinkling of rose petals, if desired.

The cake will keep in an airtight container in a cool dark place for 2–3 days.

# BOILED ORANGE MINI CAKES TOPPED WITH COCOA NIBS

*These adorable little cakes are adapted from the boiled orange chocolate cake which has been a well-loved favourite on my blog. I have left out the cocoa, instead topping the cakes with cocoa nibs for a chocolatey crunch.*

*I like to serve these delights topped with a dollop of whipped cream.*

**MAKES 12** ❖ GF, DF, VEG

Put the whole oranges in a large saucepan and cover with water. Bring to the boil, then reduce the heat and simmer for 1 hour. Drain and allow to cool.

Preheat the oven to 160°C (315°F/Gas 2–3). Grease 12 holes of a 12-hole standard muffin tin.

Cut the oranges in half and place in a food processor — skin, pith, flesh and all. Blitz until smooth.

Add the almond meal, honey, eggs and bicarbonate of soda and blitz again until smooth. Divide the batter evenly among the muffin holes, then sprinkle with the cocoa nibs.

Bake for 25–30 minutes, or until a skewer inserted in the middle of a muffin comes out clean.

Leave to cool in the tin for 10 minutes before turning out onto a wire rack.

The muffins will keep in an airtight container in a cool dark place for 2–3 days.

2 oranges
200 g (7 oz/2 cups) almond meal
4 tablespoons honey, or maple or agave syrup
5 free-range eggs
1 teaspoon bicarbonate of soda (baking soda)
35 g (1¼ oz/¼ cup) cocoa nibs, for sprinkling

# TEA-INFUSED RAISIN AND HAZELNUT CAKE

*This wonderful moist, buttery cake is inspired by a recipe of my grandmother's. The raisins are simmered with tea bags for a subtle tea infusion, then lightly sweetened with a little honey, so the spices shine through.*

*Instead of brown rice flour, you could use 100 g (3½ oz / 1 cup) spelt flour, or 130 g (4½ oz / 1 cup) buckwheat flour. This cake tastes even more beautiful a day or so after it has been made.*

**SERVES 8** ❖ GF, DF (if no butter used), VEG

170 g (5¾ oz/1 cup) raisins

3 tea bags (I prefer English breakfast, but Earl Grey also works well)

6 tablespoons honey, or maple or agave syrup

170 ml (5½ fl oz/⅔ cup) extra virgin coconut oil, or 160 g (5½ oz) unsalted butter

110 g (3¾ oz/1 cup) hazelnut meal

3 free-range eggs, lightly whisked

½ teaspoon ground nutmeg

½ teaspoon ground ginger

½ teaspoon ground cinnamon

1 teaspoon bicarbonate of soda (baking soda)

1 tablespoon apple cider vinegar

160 g (5½ oz/1 cup) brown rice flour

Put the raisins and tea bags in a small saucepan and cover with water. Bring to a gentle boil, then reduce the heat to low and simmer, uncovered, for 10–15 minutes, until almost all the water has evaporated.

Add the honey and coconut oil and stir until melted. Remove from the heat and leave to cool.

Preheat the oven to 160°C (315°F/Gas 2–3). Grease a 25 cm (10 inch) ring (bundt) tin or 20 cm (8 inch) cake tin, or line with baking paper.

Put the hazelnut meal, eggs, spices, bicarbonate of soda and vinegar in a large bowl. Sift the flour over, then add the cooled raisin mixture. Using a wooden spoon, mix until well combined.

Pour the batter into the cake tin and bake for 40–50 minutes, or until a skewer inserted in the middle of the cake comes out clean.

Leave in the tin to cool completely, before turning out onto a plate.

The cake will keep in an airtight container in a cool dark place for 4–5 days.

# LEMON AND COCONUT TRUFFLES

*If you like lemons, you'll love these truffles, made entirely from natural and nourishing ingredients — the perfect guilt-free little sweet treats.*

**MAKES ABOUT 25** ❖ GF, DF (if no butter used), VEG

180 g (6 oz/2 cups) desiccated coconut

100 g (3½ oz/1 cup) almond meal

80 ml (2½ fl oz/⅓ cup) extra virgin coconut oil, or 80 g (2¾ oz) unsalted butter

115 g (4 oz/⅓ cup) honey

grated zest and juice of 1 lemon

1 teaspoon vanilla extract

a pinch of sea salt

Set aside 45 g (1½ oz/½ cup) of the desiccated coconut in a bowl for dusting the truffles.

Put the remaining coconut in a food processor, then add the remaining ingredients and a pinch of sea salt. Blend for 1–2 minutes, until the mixture starts to come together like a dough.

Using your hands, form the mixture into small balls.

Roll the balls in the reserved coconut until well coated. Transfer to a plate, then chill in the fridge for at least 30 minutes to set.

The truffles can be kept at room temperature in an airtight container, but I find they are best kept in the fridge. They will keep for 3–4 days.

# COCONUT, BANANA AND BLACKCURRANT CAKE

*I came up with this recipe when trying to bake a healthy cake that almost all kids would enjoy. This moist, golden cake is naturally sweetened with bananas; I have added blackcurrants to give a slight tartness, but feel free to top with fruit of your choice.*

*It is perfect for a picnic, served warm with cream as a dessert, and can even be enjoyed for breakfast with a big dollop of plain yoghurt.*

**SERVES 8** ❖ GF, DF, VEG

4 free-range eggs
2 ripe bananas, peeled
185 g (6½ oz/¾ cup) nut butter (I prefer almond butter)
65 g (2¼ oz/1 cup) shredded coconut, plus extra for sprinkling over the cake
1 teaspoon bicarbonate of soda (baking soda)
75 g (2½ oz/½ cup) fresh or frozen blackcurrants

Preheat the oven to 160°C (315°F/Gas 2–3). Grease a 20 cm (8 inch) cake tin, or line with baking paper.

Blend the eggs and bananas in a food processor until smooth. Add the nut butter, coconut and bicarbonate of soda and process again until smooth.

Pour the batter into the cake tin, then sprinkle with the blackcurrants and extra coconut.

Bake for 35–40 minutes, or until a skewer inserted in the middle of the cake comes out clean.

Leave in the tin to cool completely, before turning out onto a plate.

The cake will keep in an airtight container in a cool dark place for 2–3 days.

# THE BEST NUT BUTTER CHOCOLATE

*Seriously, this is the most incredible melt-in-your-mouth chocolate. The first time I made it, our little family devoured the whole batch within a day. This rich 'chocolate' is wonderfully creamy and decadent, and made entirely with nutrient-rich ingredients.*

*I prefer to keep it in the freezer for a fudgy frozen treat, but it also keeps well in the fridge. Instead of the coconut oil, you can use cocoa butter or unsalted butter; I use almond butter in this recipe, but peanut or cashew butter would work well too. You can halve the recipe to make a smaller quantity.*

**MAKES ABOUT 15 LARGE PIECES** ❖ GF, DF, VEG, V (if no honey used)

175 g (6 oz/½ cup) honey, or 125 ml (4 fl oz/½ cup) maple or agave syrup
250 ml (9 fl oz/1 cup) extra virgin coconut oil
125 g (4½ oz/½ cup) nut butter
55 g (2 oz/½ cup) good-quality unsweetened cocoa powder

Line a 20 x 24 cm (8 x 9½ inch) slice tin with baking paper and set aside.

Melt the honey, coconut oil and nut butter together in a small saucepan over very low heat. Add the cocoa and a pinch of sea salt, then whisk until smooth.

Carefully pour into the slice tin, then place in the freezer for 1–2 hours to set.

When the mixture has set, remove it from the tin, transfer to a flat surface and carefully peel off the baking paper. Using your hands, break the mixture into bite-sized pieces.

Transfer to an airtight container. The chocolate will keep in the fridge for up to 2 weeks, or in the freezer for up to 1 month.

# ROSEMARY, OLIVE OIL AND YOGHURT CAKE

100 g (3½ oz/1 cup) almond meal
160 g (5½ oz/1 cup) rice flour, or 130 g (4½ oz/ 1 cup) buckwheat flour, or 100 g (3½ oz/1 cup) spelt flour
4 free-range eggs
grated zest of 2 lemons
200 g (7 oz/¾ cup) plain yoghurt or coconut cream
4 tablespoons honey, or maple or agave syrup
125 ml (4 fl oz/½ cup) olive oil
2 tablespoons finely chopped rosemary, plus extra leaves to garnish
1 teaspoon bicarbonate of soda (baking soda)

*This cake really couldn't be easier to make. Finely chopped rosemary adds an aromatic, rustic charm and pairs superbly with the delicate sweet tang of lemon. The yoghurt also imparts a slight tartness and beautiful moistness. This is a lovely cake to enjoy all year round.*

**SERVES 8** ❖ GF (if no spelt flour used), DF (if no yoghurt used), VEG

Preheat the oven to 150°C (300°F/Gas 2). Grease a 20 cm (8 inch) ring (bundt) tin, or line the tin with baking paper.

Put all the ingredients in a food processor and blend until smooth. Pour the batter into the cake tin, then scatter some extra rosemary over the top.

Bake for 45 minutes, or until a skewer inserted in the middle of the cake comes out clean. Leave in the tin to cool completely, before turning out onto a plate.

The cake will keep in an airtight container in a cool dark place for 3–4 days.

# FIG AND LEMON SPELT-FLOUR MUFFINS

*Figs, honey and lemon have a natural love for each other, making these deliciously light, fluffy muffins a pleasure to eat. The subtle spelt flour makes a perfect backdrop for the glorious sweetness of the figs. Enjoy in the park on a beautiful sunny day!*

**MAKES 6 MUFFINS** ❖ GF (if no spelt flour used), DF (if no butter used), VEG

2 free-range eggs

4 tablespoons honey, or maple or agave syrup

80 ml (2½ fl oz/⅓ cup) melted extra virgin coconut oil or unsalted butter

125 ml (4 fl oz/½ cup) coconut milk

200 g (7 oz/2 cups) spelt flour, or 320 g (11¼ oz/2 cups) rice flour or 260 g (9¼ oz/2 cups) buckwheat flour

1 teaspoon bicarbonate of soda (baking soda)

185 g (6½ oz/1 cup) roughly chopped dried figs

grated zest of 2 lemons

pine nuts, for sprinkling

Preheat the oven to 180°C (350°F/Gas 4). Grease six holes of a 12-hole standard muffin tin, or line with baking paper.

Put the eggs, honey, coconut oil and coconut milk in a large bowl. Whisk well, then sift in the flour and bicarbonate of soda.

Lastly, gently fold the figs and lemon zest through the batter until just combined.

Divide the mixture among the muffin holes, then sprinkle with pine nuts. Bake for 25 minutes, or until a skewer inserted in the middle of a muffin comes out clean.

Leave to cool in the tin for 10 minutes before turning out onto a wire rack.

These muffins will keep for a day or so in an airtight container, but are best eaten on the day of making. They can also be frozen for up to 2 months.

# SUNFLOWER HERB CRACKERS

*Salty, crunchy and intensely delicious, these crackers are made mostly from sunflower and sesame seeds, with a little garlic and thyme for extra kick. These must be the healthiest crackers I've ever tasted — the ideal snack when you're feeling a little peckish.*

**MAKES ABOUT 20** ❖ GF, DF, VEG, V

145 g (5 oz/1 cup) sunflower
    seeds
1 teaspoon sea salt
3 teaspoons garlic granules,
    or 3 peeled garlic cloves
75 g (2½ oz/½ cup) sesame
    seeds
1 handful of thyme leaves,
    finely chopped
1 tablespoon olive oil

Preheat the oven to 180°C (350°F/Gas 4). Line a 32 x 42 cm (12¾ x 16½ inch) baking tray with baking paper.

Put the sunflower seeds, salt and garlic in a food processor. Blend for 2–3 minutes, until the sunflower seeds take on a dense, flour-like consistency.

Add the sesame seeds, thyme and olive oil, then pulse to combine. With the motor running on low speed, slowly add 3–5 tablespoons water, one tablespoon at a time, until the mixture comes together with a dough-like consistency.

Transfer the mixture to the prepared baking tray and knead slightly — it will be a little crumbly, so don't worry. Place a sheet of baking paper on top of the dough. Using a rolling pin, roll out the dough to about 5 mm (¼ inch) thick, then remove the top sheet of baking paper. Using a sharp knife, score crisscross lines into the dough, to create about 20 crackers about 6 cm (2½ inches) square.

Bake for 10–15 minutes, or until golden brown. Allow to cool completely on the baking tray. Using your hands, break into crackers along the scored lines.

The crackers will keep in an airtight container in a cool dark place for up to 2 weeks.

# ROSEMARY, OLIVE OIL AND MAPLE SALTED NUTS

*These deliciously sweet, salty, crispy nuts can be made in less than 10 minutes. Be warned, they are addictive — highly addictive...*

**MAKES ABOUT 300 G (10½ OZ)** ❖ GF, DF, VEG, V (if no honey used)

Place a sheet of baking paper on a baking tray or wooden chopping board and set aside.

Warm the olive oil in a frying pan over medium heat. Once the oil is hot, add the nuts and rosemary and stir until the nuts are well coated — take care as the oil tends to spit a little. Keep stirring for about 2 minutes, then reduce the heat to low.

Add the maple syrup and continue to stir for a further minute. Sprinkle the salt over the nuts, then immediately remove the pan from the heat.

Using a metal spoon or spatula, transfer the nuts to the baking paper, spreading them out in a single layer to allow the syrup to harden.

Leave to cool completely, then store in an airtight container or jar. The nuts will keep in a cool dark place for 3–4 weeks.

60 ml (2 fl oz/¼ cup) extra virgin olive oil
280 g (10 oz/2 cups) mixed nuts
1 handful of rosemary leaves
3 tablespoons maple syrup, honey or agave syrup
1 teaspoon sea salt

# DRINKS

A glass of honey-sweetened blueberry lemonade makes for a refreshing beverage on a hot summer's day – or perhaps a glass of home-made peach and honey cordial topped with sparkling water and ice cubes sounds appealing. This chapter offers a lovely selection of naturally sweetened thirst-quenching drinks, as well as some that are warm, comforting and delicious, to be sipped on a chilly night.

In the colder months, why not enjoy a mug of dark spiced hot chocolate, made with creamy hazelnut milk, warming you from the inside out? I've also included a delicious recipe for a pomegranate and honey mulled wine, which I love to prepare using a beautiful bottle of vintage red wine from my father-in-law's vineyard.

# SPICED APPLE AND CINNAMON HOT TODDY

*Deliciously comforting, this warming mug of goodness tastes like cinnamon apple crumble in a cup. Be sure to use natural apple juice — organic if possible — to ensure the best quality.*

**MAKES ABOUT 1 LITRE (35 FL OZ/4 CUPS)** ❖ GF, DF, VEG, V

1 litre (35 fl oz/4 cups)
   good-quality apple juice
juice of 1 lemon
1 teaspoon ground ginger
3–4 cinnamon sticks
6 whole cloves

Put all the ingredients in a large saucepan and bring to a gentle boil over medium heat. Reduce the heat to low and simmer, stirring occasionally, for 10 minutes.

Ladle into mugs or tea cups and serve.

# POMEGRANATE AND HONEY MULLED WINE

*Pomegranate juice lends this warm, gently spiced mulled wine a slight tartness, which is perfectly rounded out with the addition of a little honey; cranberry juice also works wonderfully well instead of pomegranate juice.*

*The mulled wine is very easy to prepare — simply combine all the ingredients in a pot, then simmer until the lovely aroma of spice fills your kitchen. Serve the mulled wine while it is still warm and delicious.*

**SERVES 4** ❖ GF, DF, VEG

1 orange
750 ml (26 fl oz/3 cups) good-quality red wine
500 ml (17 fl oz/2 cups) unsweetened pomegranate juice
115 g (4 oz/⅓ cup) honey
5 cinnamon sticks
5 whole cloves
4 whole star anise
1 teaspoon ground nutmeg
1 teaspoon ground ginger

Using a vegetable peeler or sharp knife, peel long strips of zest from the orange peel, ensuring the white pith is left on the orange.

Place the orange zest strips in a large saucepan with all the remaining ingredients. Stir well to dissolve the honey, and warm slowly over low heat, being careful not to let the mixture boil. Leave to barely simmer over very low heat for 5–10 minutes.

Remove the orange zest strips. Ladle into heatproof cups or glasses and serve warm.

# DARK SPICED HOT CHOCOLATE

*This dark hot chocolate is all about spices, with cinnamon, nutmeg and cloves forming a lovely harmonious backdrop for the cocoa. I make this hot chocolate with hazelnut milk, but you could also use nut milk, oat milk, cow's milk or coconut milk.*

*It tastes just as divine served chilled on a warm day, with a few ice cubes.*

**SERVES 2** ❖ GF, DF, VEG, V (if no honey used)

2 cinnamon sticks
1 teaspoon ground nutmeg
6 whole cloves
30 g (1 oz/¼ cup) good-
    quality unsweetened
    cocoa powder
90 g (3¼ oz/¼ cup) honey,
    or 60 ml (2 fl oz/¼ cup)
    maple or agave syrup
500 ml (17 fl oz/2 cups)
    hazelnut milk

Put the cinnamon, nutmeg, cloves, cocoa and honey in a large saucepan with 250 ml (9 fl oz/1 cup) water. Bring to a gentle boil over medium heat, stirring to dissolve the honey. Reduce the heat to low and simmer for 5 minutes.

Stir in the milk and continue to heat for a minute or so, until barely simmering.

Ladle into mugs or tea cups and serve.

# PEACH AND HONEY CORDIAL

*I absolutely love this cordial. It is beautiful stirred into a glass of sparkling or still water, and can even be drizzled over yoghurt or ice cream.*

*If fresh peaches are not in season, use two 400 g (14 oz) tins of peaches preserved in naturally sweetened syrup. Drain the peaches before using.*

**MAKES ABOUT 250 ML (9 FL OZ/1 CUP)** ❖ GF, DF, VEG, V (if no honey used)

juice of 1 lemon
5 peaches, peeled, stoned
   and chopped
175 g (6 oz/½ cup) honey,
   or 125 ml (4 fl oz/¼ cup)
   maple or agave syrup

Combine the lemon juice, peaches and honey in a large saucepan with 500 ml (17 fl oz/2 cups) water. Bring to the boil over medium heat, then reduce the heat to low. Simmer for 45 minutes, or until the liquid has reduced by half.

Strain the syrup through muslin (cheesecloth) or a very fine mesh sieve, into a sterilised glass bottle or jar.

To serve, add 3 parts still or sparkling water to 1 part cordial; you can adjust these ratios to suit your taste.

The cordial will keep in the fridge for 3–4 days.

# MINT AND LEMON SUN-BREWED TEA

*This slightly different technique for brewing tea requires only the natural sunlight on your back porch or kitchen window sill, and a 1 litre (35 fl oz / 4 cup) glass jar. Once the tea has steeped, add a few ice cubes, then sit back and enjoy this refreshing and lovely iced infusion.*

**SERVES 3–4** ❖ GF, DF, VEG, V (if no honey used)

4 tea bags of your choice
1 large handful of mint
   leaves
1 lemon, sliced into rounds
1–2 tablespoons honey, or
   maple or agave syrup
   (optional)
1 litre (35 fl oz/4 cups) filtered
   water

Sterilise your jar by boiling it in a large saucepan of water for 10 minutes. Making sun-brewed tea provides ideal conditions for bacterial growth, so this step is very important.

Add the tea bags, mint, lemon and honey, if using, to the jar. Stir together, then pour the filtered water in.

Seal the jar, place in a sunny spot and leave to steep for 2–3 hours.

Strain into cups and enjoy with a few ice cubes.

# BLUEBERRY AND HONEY SPARKLING LEMONADE

*A sparkling lemonade to quench your thirst on a hot summer's day. Sweetened with honey, it also has a lovely fresh citrus kick from the lemon juice. Try to use organic lemons if possible, for their wonderful juice.*

*This version is topped with sparkling water, but still water would work nicely also.*

**SERVES 6** ❖ GF, DF, VEG, V (if no honey used)

250 ml (9 fl oz/1 cup) freshly squeezed lemon juice
115 g (4 oz/⅓ cup) honey, or 80 ml (2½ fl oz/⅓ cup) maple or agave syrup
310 g (11 oz/2 cups) blueberries, plus an extra 80 g (2¾ oz/½ cup) blueberries, to serve
1 litre (35 fl oz/4 cups) sparkling or soda water

Pour the lemon juice and 250 ml (9 fl oz/1 cup) water into a small saucepan. Stir in the honey and add the 310 g (11 oz/2 cups) of blueberries. Bring to a gentle boil over medium heat, then reduce the heat to low and simmer for 5 minutes. Remove from the heat and leave to cool.

Strain through a sieve, into a large jug or pitcher, then top with the sparkling water.

Pour into serving glasses, and add an ice cube or two to each glass. Add the extra blueberries and serve.

# PEANUT BUTTER MILKSHAKE

*Sweetened with a little honey and banana, this delightfully nutty milkshake has a thick, creamy texture from the peanut butter. I like to drink it in the afternoon for a healthy dose of protein to get me through the rest of the day.*

*Oat milk, cow's milk, nut milk and coconut milk all work well in this delicious milkshake — definitely a 'must try'!*

**SERVES 2–3** ❖ GF, DF (if no dairy milk used), VEG, V (if no dairy milk or honey used)

1 ripe banana, peeled
500 ml (17 fl oz/2 cups) milk of your choice
90 g (3¼ oz/⅓ cup) peanut butter
2 tablespoons honey, or maple or agave syrup
4–5 ice cubes

Put all the ingredients in a blender and blend until smooth. Pour into glasses and enjoy!

# VANILLA, CINNAMON AND DATE MILKSHAKE

*An after-school favourite in our household, this simple milkshake is wonderfully creamy, and also has a slight caramel taste from the dates.*

*It can be dairy-free depending on your choice of milk; I prefer organic full-cream cow's milk, but have also used half coconut water and half coconut cream, which tastes divine too. Nut, oat and coconut milk work well also.*

**SERVES 2–3** ❖ GF, DF (if no dairy milk used), VEG, V (if no dairy milk used)

500 ml (17 fl oz/2 cups) milk of your choice
10 pitted medjool dates
1 teaspoon ground cinnamon
2 teaspoons vanilla extract
8–10 ice cubes

Put all the ingredients in a blender and blend until smooth. Pour into glasses and enjoy!

# BERRY AND CHOCOLATE SMOOTHIE

150 g (5½ oz/1 cup) fresh
  or frozen berries of your
  choice, plus an extra 75 g
  (2½ oz/½ cup) berries,
  to serve (optional)
flesh of 1 avocado, roughly
  chopped
8 pitted medjool dates
500 ml (17 fl oz/2 cups)
  coconut milk
40 g (1½ oz/⅓ cup) good-
  quality unsweetened
  cocoa powder
2 tablespoons cocoa nibs, to
  serve (optional)

*The chocolate and berries work fantastically together in this thick, silky smoothie. I like to use coconut milk, as it gives such a creamy, sumptuous texture, but you could also use oat, nut or cow's milk.*

*This smoothie really does taste so beautiful, you won't believe it's good for you.*

**SERVES 2** ❖ GF, DF, VEG, V

Put the 150 g (5½ oz/1 cup) of berries in a blender. Add the avocado, dates, coconut milk and cocoa powder and blend until smooth.

Pour into glasses. Top with extra berries, if desired, and serve sprinkled with the cocoa nibs.

# PEAR, CUCUMBER AND GINGER JUICE

*This refreshing juice is both light and sweet, and can be served over ice if desired. Ginger is a natural detoxifier and immunity booster and helps soothe an upset stomach.*

**SERVES 2** ❖ GF, DF, VEG, V

2 pears
1 Lebanese (short) cucumber
1 small handful of flat-leaf (Italian) parsley
1 thumb-sized piece of fresh ginger, peeled

Pass all the ingredients through an electric juicer.

If you don't have a juicer, put all the ingredients in a blender with 500 ml (17 fl oz/2 cups) water. Blend for a minute or so, then pass the juice through a fine-mesh sieve, into a jug or pitcher.

Pour into glasses, then enjoy immediately, while the juice is still very fresh.

# BEETROOT, APPLE AND ACAI BERRY JUICE

*Acai berry adds an extra dose of antioxidants, vitamins, minerals and omega plant oils to this healthy juice.*

**SERVES 2** ❖ GF, DF, VEG, V

1 beetroot (beet), scrubbed thoroughly
3 apples
2 teaspoons dried acai berry powder

Pass the beetroot and apples through an electric juicer.

If you don't have a juicer, roughly chop the beetroot and apples and place in a blender with 750 ml (26 fl oz/3 cups) water. Blend for a minute or so, then pass the juice through a fine-mesh sieve, into a jug or pitcher.

Pour the juice into two glasses, then stir 1 teaspoon acai berry powder into each glass.

Add a few ice cubes if desired, then enjoy immediately, while the juice is still very fresh.

# BASICS

The following pages bring together a handful of
simple recipes that I use in my day-to-day cooking
— covering everything from beautiful home-made
stocks, ghee and nut milk to raw chia seed jam and
honey-sweetened lemon curd. I much prefer these
home-made delights to the store-bought versions,
because I know they are as natural and wholesome as
possible. These recipes also make wonderful building
blocks to many delicious meals.

# HOME-MADE MEAT STOCK

*At the start of each week, I make a large batch of meat stock. Slow-cooked meat stock contains a large amount of vitamins and minerals, and is extremely nourishing for the body and digestive system.*

*This lovely home-made stock can be made using beef, ham or chicken bones and adds tremendous flavour to dishes. I like to use the left-over bones from a roast, which give a deep aromatic flavour.*

*Feel free to add your favourite vegetables and herbs, to give the stock that little bit extra.*

**MAKES 3–4 LITRES (105–140 FL OZ/12–16 CUPS)** ❖ GF, DF (if no ghee or butter used)

1 large free-range chicken carcass, raw or previously cooked, or 1 kg (2 lb 4 oz) beef or lamb bones

2 tablespoons ghee, butter or olive oil

2–3 carrots, roughly chopped

2–3 celery stalks, roughly chopped

1 garlic bulb, each clove peeled and lightly smashed

1 fennel bulb, tough outer layer discarded, inner part roughly chopped

1 leek, white part only, roughly chopped

1 large handful of herbs, such as thyme, rosemary and sage

2–3 bay leaves

2 teaspoons sea salt

Put all the ingredients in a stockpot or very large saucepan, along with some freshly ground black pepper. Pour in enough water to cover the bones and bring to a gentle boil.

Reduce the heat to low. Simmer for at least 2 hours, or longer if you have time, adding more water if needed.

Taste and adjust the seasonings if necessary. Remove the meat and vegetables if you prefer, then strain the stock through a sieve, into a large clean saucepan or heatproof bowl.

Allow to cool, then transfer to smaller containers. The stock will keep in the fridge for up to 1 week, or in the freezer for up to 6 months in freezer-proof containers.

NOTE ⟫⟫⟫

You can also make this stock overnight using a slow cooker. Just put all the ingredients in the slow cooker, press the button and cook on low for 6–8 hours.

# HOME-MADE VEGETABLE STOCK

*I like to add a few large handfuls of herbs and a whole garlic bulb while simmering this beautifully aromatic stock. It is fantastic for imparting deep, delicious flavour to all manner of vegetarian dishes.*

**MAKES 3–4 LITRES (105–140 FL OZ/12–16 CUPS)** ❖ GF, DF (if no ghee or butter used), VEG, V (if no ghee or butter used)

2 tablespoons ghee, butter or olive oil
1 large onion, roughly chopped
2–3 carrots, roughly chopped
2–3 celery stalks, roughly chopped
1 fennel bulb, roughly chopped
1 leek, roughly chopped
1 garlic bulb, each clove peeled and roughly chopped
1 large handful of herbs, such as thyme, rosemary and sage
2–3 bay leaves
2 teaspoons sea salt

Melt the ghee in a stockpot or very large saucepan over medium heat. Add the vegetables and garlic and sauté for 10 minutes, or until lightly browned and soft.

Add the remaining ingredients, along with some freshly ground black pepper. Cover with water and bring to a gentle boil.

Reduce the heat to low. Simmer for at least 2 hours, or longer if you have time, adding more water if needed.

Taste and adjust the seasonings if necessary. Remove the vegetables if you prefer, then strain the stock through a sieve, into a large clean saucepan or heatproof bowl.

Allow to cool, then transfer to smaller containers. The stock will keep in the fridge for up to 1 week, or in the freezer for up to 6 months in freezer-proof containers.

NOTE ⟫⟫⟫
You can also make this stock overnight using a slow cooker. Just put all the ingredients in the slow cooker, press the button and cook on low for 6–8 hours.

# SIMPLE BASIL AND GARLIC TOMATO SAUCE

*With a rich and slightly sweet taste from the basil, this thick, pulpy tomato sauce is a staple in many of my recipes. It is so easy to prepare — simply place all the ingredients in a saucepan and simmer until doubled in flavour.*

**MAKES ABOUT 1 LITRE (35 FL OZ/4 CUPS)** ❖ GF, DF, VEG, V

3 x 400 g (14 oz) tins whole or chopped tomatoes
5 garlic cloves, roughly chopped
2 large handfuls of basil leaves, roughly chopped

Place the tomatoes, garlic and basil in a large saucepan, season with sea salt and freshly ground black pepper and mix until well combined.

Bring to a gentle boil, then reduce the heat to low, cover and gently simmer for 25–30 minutes, or until the sauce is thick and pulpy.

Leave to cool, then transfer to a sterilised glass jar.

The sauce will keep in the fridge for up to 1 week.

# HOME-MADE GHEE

*Ghee (also known as clarified butter) is a ridiculously rich and flavourful version of regular butter, with beautiful nutty notes. It has been used in Ayurvedic medicine for hundreds of years for its healing qualities.*

*Ghee can be cooked at a higher smoke point and for a longer time than regular butter or oil, so a small jar of ghee is nice to have on hand for scrambling eggs or sautéing meats, fish and vegetables in a frying pan — or even for stirring into a comforting pot of just-cooked mash.*

**MAKES ABOUT 350 ML (12 FL OZ)** ❖ GF, VEG

Melt the butter in a saucepan over very low heat. Simmer gently for 4–5 minutes, until the foam rises to the top. The butter may splutter a little, so be careful.

Once the butter stops spluttering, and no more foam seems to be rising to the surface, remove from the heat and skim off the foam with a spoon. You will know the butter is ready, as it will give off a beautiful nutty smell.

Line a sieve with a few layers of muslin (cheesecloth) or gauze, then set the sieve over a heatproof bowl or glass jar.

Carefully pour the ghee through the sieve, leaving behind any solids from the bottom of the pan.

The ghee will keep in a sterilised jar in a cool dark place for up to 3 months, or up to 1 year in the fridge.

500 g (1 lb 2 oz) organic unsalted butter

# THE BEST MUSTARD VINAIGRETTE

*This simple vinaigrette is great as a salad dressing and fantastic drizzled over roasted vegetables and meat. It has the most harmonious balance of flavours — a tangy kick from the balsamic vinegar and a lovely hum of garlic.*

*Feel free to tweak the recipe to suit your taste. If you're a vegan or vegetarian, you can omit the worcestershire sauce.*

**MAKES ABOUT 220 ML (7½ FL OZ)** ❖ GF, DF

125 ml (4 fl oz/½ cup) extra virgin olive oil
80 ml (2½ fl oz/⅓ cup) balsamic vinegar
1 tablespoon dijon mustard
2 teaspoons worcestershire sauce
1 garlic clove, finely chopped

Put all the ingredients in a clean jar, along with a generous pinch of sea salt and freshly ground black pepper. Screw the lid on tightly and shake well.

Taste the vinaigrette, then adjust the flavour by adding a little more of any of the ingredients as desired.

The vinaigrette will keep in a sterilised jar in the fridge for about 2 weeks, but is best served at room temperature.

# SPINACH, LEMON ZEST AND CASHEW PESTO

*This is a simple yet delicious dairy-free version of the classic pesto, using rich, creamy cashew nuts instead of the usual parmesan cheese.*

*Full of punch, it is sublime tossed through salads, added to roasted vegetables, and slathered over fish or chicken.*

**MAKES ENOUGH FOR A 350 ML (12 FL OZ) JAR** ❖ GF, DF, VEG, V

80 g (2¾ oz/½ cup) cashew nuts
125 ml (4 fl oz/½ cup) extra virgin olive oil
1 large handful of flat-leaf (Italian) parsley or basil leaves
1 large handful of baby English spinach leaves
zest and juice of 1 lemon
2 garlic cloves, peeled

Put all the ingredients in a food processor with a large pinch of sea salt and freshly ground black pepper.

Process until a thick, chunky pesto consistency is reached. Taste and add a little more olive oil, lemon juice or seasoning as desired.

The pesto will keep in a sterilised jar in the fridge for up to 1 week.

# CREAMY YOGHURT CHEESE

*Incredibly simple to make, this cheese has a smooth creamy and tangy taste, with a subtle acidic note, making it perfect for both savoury and sweet dishes.*

*It is lovely served on its own with honey and fresh fruit, but you can experiment by adding your favourite herbs and spices. I like to add a sprinkling of thyme and lemon zest.*

**MAKES ABOUT 260 G (9¼ OZ/1 CUP)** ❖ GF, VEG

520 g (1 lb 2½ oz/2 cups) plain yoghurt

Line a sieve with two large pieces of muslin (cheesecloth), then set the sieve over a large bowl.

Put the yoghurt on the cloth and sprinkle with a large pinch of sea salt. Twist together the corners of the cloth, like a money bag.

Place a small plate on top, then weigh down with a tin of food or something similar.

Refrigerate overnight. The longer you leave the yoghurt, the more liquid will drip away and the drier the cheese will become.

The cheese will keep in a sterilised jar in the fridge for up to 2 weeks.

# LEMON ZEST AND GARLIC AÏOLI

*This rich, creamy aïoli is a magical accompaniment to many dishes, with its lovely buzz of garlic and zesty lemon kick. I love drizzling it over crispy roasted vegetables.*

**MAKES ABOUT 310 G (11 OZ/1¼ CUPS)** ❖ GF, DF, VEG

2 free-range egg yolks,
   at room temperature
2 garlic cloves, roughly
   chopped
zest and juice of 1 lemon
250 ml (9 fl oz/1 cup) fruity
   olive oil

Put the egg yolks, garlic and lemon zest in a blender. Add a pinch of sea salt and freshly ground black pepper.

Begin to blend on low and start to pour in the olive oil in a slow, steady trickle. You will know the aïoli is ready when the consistency begins to resemble a thick, glossy mayonnaise.

Lastly, add the lemon juice. Taste and adjust the seasonings if needed.

The aïoli will keep in a sterilised jar in the fridge for 3–4 days.

# HONEY WHIPPED COCONUT CREAM

*Containing only three simple ingredients, this dairy-free whipped topping is luscious, thick and creamy... just begging to be added to your favourite dessert, or serving alongside baked sweet treats. It takes very little time to prepare, although you will need to start this recipe several hours in advance, or preferably the night before.*

**MAKES 500 ML (17 FL OZ/2 CUPS)** ❖ GF, DF, VEG, V (if no honey used)

Start by placing the tins of coconut cream in the fridge for at least 6 hours, or preferably overnight, so the thickest part of the coconut cream separates from the coconut water.

When you remove the tins from the fridge, be careful not to shake them, or move them around at all. Carefully open the tins, then scoop the thickened cream from the top, into a mixing bowl. The amount of thickened cream may vary in each tin, but I'm usually able to scoop out around half a tin each. Reserve the remaining liquid to use in a smoothie.

Add the honey to the thickened coconut cream, and the vanilla if using. Beat well with an egg beater for 5 minutes, or until the cream is lovely and thick, and slightly fluffier in texture.

The cream will keep in an airtight container in the fridge for up to 1 week.

2 x 400 ml (14 fl oz) tins
   organic coconut cream
1 tablespoon honey, or agave
   or maple syrup
1 teaspoon pure vanilla
   extract (optional)

# HONEY-ROASTED NUT BUTTER WITH SEA SALT

*This rich nut butter has the perfect balance of sweet and saltiness, blended to creamy, slightly crunchy perfection; vanilla extract and ground cinnamon and nutmeg are also lovely additions. Once you taste it, you'll never want to buy the commercially produced versions again.*

**MAKES ABOUT 350 G (12 OZ/2 CUPS)** ❖ GF, DF (if no ghee or butter used), VEG, V (if no honey, ghee or butter used)

310 g (11 oz/2 cups) raw organic nuts or seeds
2 tablespoons honey, or agave or maple syrup
1 teaspoon sea salt
2 tablespoons extra virgin coconut oil, ghee, butter or olive oil

Preheat the oven to 180°C (350°F/Gas 4). Line a large baking tray with baking paper.

Combine the nuts, honey and sea salt in a mixing bowl. Using your hands, mix well so that all the nuts are evenly coated. Spread the nuts out in one layer over the baking tray.

Bake for 10–15 minutes, or until lovely and golden. Remove from the oven and leave to cool.

Put the nuts in a food processor and process for 1–2 minutes, until a crumb-like consistency is reached. Add the coconut oil, then process for a further 2–3 minutes, until the butter has the desired level of smoothness (I prefer mine slightly crunchy).

Taste and add a little more salt if needed.

Transfer to a sterilised glass jar and seal. The nut butter will keep in a cool dark place for 2–3 months.

# RAW DATE SYRUP

*With its beautiful sweet caramel taste, this syrup is a fantastic natural sweetener. Use it in baking and smoothies, or drizzle it over yoghurt or desserts.*

**MAKES 375–500 ML (13–17 FL OZ/1½–2 CUPS)** ❖ GF, DF, VEG, V

160 g (5½ oz/1 cup) pitted medjool dates
juice of ½ lemon
1 teaspoon vanilla extract (optional)

Put the dates, lemon juice and vanilla extract, if using, in a blender with a pinch of sea salt and 125–250 ml (4–9 fl oz/½–1 cup) water.

Process for a few minutes, until you have a smooth syrup. Add a little more water if needed.

The syrup will keep in a sterilised glass jar in the fridge for up to 3 weeks.

# SEA SALT AND HERB PRESERVED LEMONS

*Preserving lemons removes their bitterness. The skin is delicious with chicken and fish, tossed through sautéed vegetables, or mashed into butter with fresh herbs.*

**MAKES 6–8 PRESERVED LEMONS** ❖ GF, DF, VEG, V

Place 2 tablespoons of the salt in the bottom of a large sterilised jar, about 1 litre (35 fl oz/4 cups) in capacity.

Slice 1–2 cm (½–¾ inch) off the tip of each lemon. Starting from the top, make a deep cut into each lemon, but do not cut all the way down — keep the lemons attached at the base. Make another cut in a similar manner, at a 90-degree angle to the first cut, so the lemons are now quartered, but still attached at the base.

Prise the lemons open, then generously sprinkle salt all over the insides and outsides.

Stack the lemons in the jar, alternating them with the herbs, and squashing the lemons down to extract all the juice. Fill the jar with the lemons, making sure the top is covered with lemon juice, and adding extra lemon juice if needed. Top with a couple of tablespoons of salt.

Seal the jar and leave to sit at room temperature for 2–3 weeks, turning the jar upside down occasionally.

To use, remove a lemon from the jar and rinse lightly to remove the salt. (I usually use a whole lemon at a time; for a smaller amount, cut off whatever portion you need and return the unrinsed remainder to the salty brine.) Discard any flesh, then thinly slice or dice the skin.

The lemons will keep in the fridge for up to 1 year.

65 g (2¼ oz/½ cup) sea salt, more if needed

6–8 organic lemons, stems removed

1 large handful of fresh herbs, such as mint, thyme, rosemary or parsley

extra freshly squeezed lemon juice, if needed

# RAW CHIA SEED JAM

*This jam takes all of five minutes to prepare, and requires no cooking. I love that it contains no refined sugar. The secret ingredient is the super-nutritious chia seeds, which absorb water to give a jelly, jam-like consistency. Serve it on toast, just like a regular fruit jam, spoon it over yoghurt, and use it in baking.*

*Feel free to experiment with this recipe; I've made the jam using many different types of berries and fruit.*

**MAKES ABOUT 400 G (14 OZ/2½ CUPS)** ❖ GF, DF, VEG, V (if no honey used)

250 g (9 oz/2 cups) frozen or chopped fresh fruit
2 tablespoons honey, or maple or agave syrup (optional)
30 g (1 oz/¼ cup) chia seeds

Put the fruit in a food processor or blender. Add 60 ml (2 fl oz/¼ cup) water, and the honey if using. Pulse together until just blended.

Transfer to a sterilised glass jar, then add the chia seeds and mix well, making sure they are well incorporated into the fruit.

Place in the fridge to set for at least 1 hour.

The jam will keep in the fridge for 2–3 weeks.

# CREAMY OAT MILK

*This home-made oat milk has a slightly nutty taste and silky-smooth texture. It is perfectly creamy, making it a wonderful dairy-free alternative. Add a little honey, cinnamon, cocoa or vanilla extract for a lovely flavoured milk.*

**MAKES ABOUT 1 LITRE (35 FL OZ/4 CUPS)** ❖ GF, DF, VEG, V

Rinse the oats in a colander, then place in a blender with the remaining ingredients. Add a pinch of sea salt and process for 1–2 minutes, or until smooth.

Leave the milk to rest for 1 hour.

Strain the milk through a fine sieve, into a sterilised glass jar. You can repeat this step two or three times to remove all the grains. If you are worried about waste, reserve the left-over pulpy grains to fold into a cake or muffin batter.

The milk will keep in the fridge for 4–5 days. It will separate as it sits, so simply stir or shake before using.

25 g (1 oz/¼ cup) rolled (porridge) oats, soaked in water overnight
4–6 pitted medjool dates, soaked in water overnight
1 litre (35 fl oz/4 cups) filtered water

# NUT MILK

*Another fantastic dairy-free alternative, and deliciously creamy and nourishing. I have made this milk using almonds, cashew nuts, hazelnuts and brazil nuts — all versions are equally beautiful.*

**MAKES ABOUT 1 LITRE (35 FL OZ/4 CUPS)** ❖ GF, DF, VEG, V

310 g (11 oz/2 cups) raw nuts, soaked in water overnight, then drained
6 pitted medjool dates, soaked in water overnight
1 litre (35 fl oz/4 cups) filtered water

Place all the ingredients in a blender and pulse until the nuts are pulverised.

Leave the milk to rest for 30 minutes, then strain through a fine sieve, into a sterilised glass jar. If you are worried about waste, reserve the left-over nut pulp to fold into a cake or muffin batter.

The milk will keep in the fridge for 2–3 days.

# COCONUT CARAMEL SAUCE

*Naturally sweetened, this sauce is wonderfully thick, creamy and spreadable — marvellous for topping cakes, filling biscuits or cookies, drizzling over desserts, and of course eating with a spoon!*

**MAKES ABOUT 500 ML (17 FL OZ/2 CUPS)** ❖ GF, DF, VEG, V (if no honey used)

400 ml (14 fl oz) tin full-fat coconut cream
175 g (6 oz/½ cup) honey, or 125 ml (4 fl oz/½ cup) maple or agave syrup

Put the coconut cream, honey and a pinch of sea salt in a saucepan over medium heat and stir to combine.

Bring to a gentle boil, then reduce the heat to low. Simmer for 20–30 minutes, or until the mixture is a lovely golden caramel colour. Stir often towards the end as the sauce can burn easily.

Remove from the heat and leave to cool slightly. Stir vigorously for a minute or so and watch the sauce become nice and thick.

Pour into a sterilised glass jar. The sauce will keep in the fridge for about 1 week.

# LEMON CURD

*Heavenly smooth and creamy, this tangy curd is dairy free and contains only nourishing and wholesome ingredients. Swirl it into ice cream, yoghurt or whipped cream, smother it on top of your favourite cake, pancakes or dessert... the possibilities are vast.*

**MAKES ABOUT 350 ML (12 FL OZ)** ❖ GF, DF (if no butter used), VEG

80 ml (2½ fl oz/⅓ cup) extra virgin coconut oil, or melted unsalted butter
4 tablespoons honey, or maple or agave syrup
4 free-range eggs, lightly beaten
125 ml (4 fl oz/½ cup) freshly squeezed lemon juice; you'll need about 5 lemons

Put the coconut oil and honey in a small saucepan and melt together over low heat. Remove from the heat and leave to cool.

Add the eggs and lemon juice, then whisk until well combined.

Place back over low heat, then continue to whisk for 2–3 minutes, or until the curd becomes lovely and thick and small bubbles start to pop at the surface. Carefully pour into a sterilised glass jar.

The lemon curd will keep in the fridge for up to 1 week.

# INDEX

Page numbers in *italics* refer to photographs.

# ACKNOWLEDGEMENTS

*Thank you to my wonderful husband,* and to my two beautiful children. Izabella and Obi, you are an endless inspiration to me. Nothing brings me more joy than to prepare nourishing and healthy food for you. Valentin, you are my rock, my best friend and the most supportive husband I could ever ask for. I love you more than words can describe.

To my beautiful family and friends — there are too many of you to thank separately. You have offered incredible amounts of loving support, encouragement and words of wisdom. Thank you for being there when I needed you. You are amazing, and I love you all.

A massive thank you to the brilliant team at Murdoch Books, for seeing the potential in me, and in this beautiful publication. I feel honoured to have been able to work with you all. It has been an absolute joy.

A special thank you to my blog readers. Your support and positive feedback have been invaluable, and without you all, this book would not have been possible.

Much love, hugs and kisses to you all.

Published in 2014 by Murdoch Books, an imprint of Allen & Unwin.
Reprinted 2014 (twice), 2015

Murdoch Books Australia
83 Alexander Street
Crows Nest NSW 2065
Phone: +61 (0) 2 8425 0100
Fax: +61 (0) 2 9906 2218
www.murdochbooks.com.au
info@murdochbooks.com.au

Murdoch Books UK
Erico House, 6th Floor
93–99 Upper Richmond Road
Putney, London SW15 2TG
Phone: +44 (0) 20 8785 5995
www.murdochbooks.co.uk
info@murdochbooks.co.uk

For Corporate Orders & Custom Publishing contact Noel Hammond,
National Business Development Manager, Murdoch Books Australia

Publisher: Corinne Roberts
Photographer and Stylist: Eleanor Ozich
Food Editor: Katy Holder
Editor: Katri Hilden
Designer: Katy Wall
Editorial Manager: Claire Grady
Design Manager: Hugh Ford
Production Manager: Karen Small

Text and photography copyright © Eleanor Ozich 2014
Design copyright © Murdoch Books 2014

The images on the back cover and pages 6, 133, 152, 153 and 227 were photographed by Gem
Adams. All other images by Eleanor Ozich.

A cataloguing-in-publication entry is available from the catalogue of the National Library of
Australia at www.nla.gov.au.

A catalogue record for this book is available from the British Library.

Colour reproduction by Splitting Image, Clayton, Victoria.

Printed by Hang Tai Printing Company Limited, China.

IMPORTANT: Those who might be at risk from the effects of salmonella poisoning (the elderly,
pregnant women, young children and those suffering from immune deficiency diseases) should
consult their doctor with any concerns about eating raw eggs.

OVEN GUIDE: You may find cooking times vary depending on the oven you are using. We have used
a fan-forced oven in these recipes. As a general rule, set the temperature for a conventional oven 20°C
(35°F) higher than indicated in the recipe.

MEASURES GUIDE: We have used 20 ml (4 teaspoon) tablespoon measures. If you are using a 15 ml
(3 teaspoon) tablespoon add an extra teaspoon of the ingredient for each tablespoon specified.